MW00903104

Isaiah 58:6-12

You will be a
rebuilder of walls,
restorer of homes.

Having watched firsthand the impact that the mission field experience had on Paul and Stephanie served as a tremendous blessing to me! This book speaks to the importance of why missions like Sports Outreach encourage as many as we can to take the step into the unknown, shed the surroundings of their current environment, present themselves as a tool for loving service, still their mind and heart to hear God speak and watch how God allows them to fulfill His purpose in their life.

—Sal Ferlise, CEO Sports Outreach Institute

Morpheus said accurately to Neo in the movie The Matrix "There is a difference between knowing the path and walking the path." In "Called to Follow" author Paul McDonald has masterfully shared his journey of "walking the path" with Jesus. Readers will be inspired and challenged by Paul's heart felt stories from his ministry work in Africa while also being instructed on practical steps to follow their personal calling. Read and respond to "Called to Follow" and begin to experience for yourself that there is a difference, a life changing difference, from simply "knowing the path" and "walking the path" with Jesus.

—Dan Horner,
Founding Partner-True Homes and
Founder of Mission Uprising

Paul McDonald's engaging account of his time in Uganda reflects actual events and people is a world far removed from Western society and culture. The reader will enjoy seeing this world through Paul's first-hand experience, as he describes his encounters with various people during his medical missions trip. Even more, Paul will challenge the reader to consider the many ministry possibilities God provides. His honest, down-to-earth approach will encourage his readers to consider how God can use them in their everyday world—or perhaps even in a far away place like Uganda.

—Dr. Tim Hoke,
African Bible University

Called to Follow is a sincere and challenging account of the extraordinary things God can do through us when we are willing to follow His call. Paul McDonald's honesty in sharing his triumphs and struggles while serving in Africa are telling and insightful. Regardless of whether we wish to serve locally or abroad, this book challenges us to let go of idols of comfort to reach towards the calling God has always intended for us.

—Kelly Griffin,
Former World Race Missionary
with Adventures in Missions

CALLED
TO FOLLOW

PAUL McDONALD

WESTBOW
PRESS®
A DIVISION OF THOMAS NELSON
& ZONDERVAN

Copyright © 2016 Paul McDonald.

All rights reserved. No part of this book may be used or reproduced by
any means, graphic, electronic, or mechanical, including photocopying,
recording, taping or by any information storage retrieval system
without the written permission of the author except in the case of
brief quotations embodied in critical articles and reviews.

WestBow Press books may be ordered through booksellers or by contacting:

WestBow Press
A Division of Thomas Nelson & Zondervan
1663 Liberty Drive
Bloomington, IN 47403
www.westbowpress.com
1 (866) 928-1240

Because of the dynamic nature of the Internet, any web addresses or
links contained in this book may have changed since publication and
may no longer be valid. The views expressed in this work are solely those
of the author and do not necessarily reflect the views of the publisher,
and the publisher hereby disclaims any responsibility for them.

Any people depicted in stock imagery provided by Thinkstock are models,
and such images are being used for illustrative purposes only.
Certain stock imagery © Thinkstock.

ISBN: 978-1-9736-0163-0 (sc)
ISBN: 978-1-9736-0164-7 (hc)
ISBN: 978-1-9736-0162-3 (e)

Library of Congress Control Number: 2017913841

Print information available on the last page.

WestBow Press rev. date: 10/02/2017

This book is a work of non-fiction. Unless otherwise noted, the author and the publisher make no explicit guarantees as to the accuracy of the information contained in this book and in some cases, names of people and places have been altered to protect their privacy.

Scripture quotations marked (NIV) are taken from the Holy Bible, New International Version®, NIV®. Copyright © 1973, 1978, 1984, 2011 by Biblica, Inc.™ Used by permission of Zondervan. All rights reserved worldwide. www.zondervan.com The "NIV" and "New International Version" are trademarks registered in the United States Patent and Trademark Office by Biblica, Inc.™ The Holy Bible, English Standard Version® (ESV®) Copyright © 2001 by Crossway, a publishing ministry of Good News Publishers. All rights reserved. ESV Text Edition: 2016 Scripture quotations marked HCSB are from the Holman Christian Standard Bible®. HCSB®. Copyright © 1999, 2000, 2002, 2003 by Holman Bible Publishers. Used by permission. Holman Christian Standard Bible™, Holman CSB™, and HCSB™ are federally registered trademarks of Holman Bible Publishers.

Artist Name for interior credit: Bishop Beall (photos), Leigh Ann Loblein (photos), Scott Brinkley (header images)

Dedication

This book is dedicated to my wonderful wife, partner, and best friend Stephanie. You kept me going when I didn't think I could do it anymore. You always believe the best in me. I am so thankful for our adventures together, and look forward to many more.

I love you.

Acknowledgments

I have to start out by thanking my good friend, Bishop (this is his first name, not his title) Beall. Without your invitation, vision, and friendship, this trip would not have happened. Without the trip, this book doesn't happen. You are my battle buddy. You always have my back, and I am so thankful for your friendship.

I need to mention our team that went to Uganda in February 2015: Kristy Beall, Sal Ferlise, Reuben and Kim Villareal, Jimmy and Missy Trent, Tom and Leigh Ann Loeblein, Steve Peterson, Stacy Sannem, Brittany Barclay, Mike Hadnagy, Angie Shepherd, Karen Geiger, Jennifer Farres, Angela Darket, Hal and Pam Guice, George Caylor, and Dave Pelfrey. You guys are my family, and we saw and accomplished many things on this amazing trip. I'm so glad to know each of you.

This trip would not have happened without our support teams at Bless Back Worldwide and Sports Outreach Institute/ Ministry. You do amazing work, and I am so thankful to partner with you and walk alongside you. I especially want to thank Robert Katende for being willing to write the foreword to this book. I can't imagine how busy you must have been at that time. Words cannot express the appreciation I have for your willingness to participate with me. I also want to thank our hosts in Uganda: Sam, Wilfred, Phiona Mutesi, Fred and Nicolette Barungi, Lydia, Moses, Patrick, Aloysius, Esther, Denis, Paul, Sophie, Prossy, Sam, Rodney, Juventan, Jimmy and all the other volunteers who worked with us that week.

I love my Writer's Boot Camp community. The teachings from Margaret Feinberg and Jonathan Merritt transformed my writing. Kurt Ward (extra thanks for your help with editing), David Ellis, and Ryan Sanders—I am so grateful for your friendship, leadership, encouragement, and support. This book is here because of your input and direction.

I want to recognize Scott Brinkley for his help and support for this book. Your creative insight and work put pictures to my words, showing things in ways that are impossible for me. I look forward to seeing what God has in store for us.

I could not have written this without my band of brothers to support and encourage me as well. Thanks to Randy Angel, Jeb Buchan, Bill Browning, Dan Horner, Chris Stater, John Anderson, Ricky Furr, Eric Bird and Patrick Creehan. I could not ask for a better group of men to walk this path with me. You are my spiritual Spartans!

I would like to thank Tina Ralyea for always believing in me and encouraging me, giving me opportunities to grow, and seeing potential where others did not.

Any acknowledgments would be empty without recognizing my parents, Paul and Linda McDonald. I love you both and am so thankful for your support and love through this roller-coaster life of mine. I don't know where I would be without your voices in my life. Dad, thanks for reading this and giving me some tough feedback. I appreciate your input, even when we don't agree.

To my brother Mike—I'm so thankful for you, and excited to continue our mission in Uganda. God has done amazing things in your life (such as your wife/my sis, Jess, and your five awesome kids—Austin, Ellie, Callie, Suzie and Chris). I am eager to watch God continue to use you to accomplish His purposes here on earth. I look forward to living life together.

I want to thank my children: Zack, Lanie, Brendan and Andrew. You guys gave up a great deal so Stephanie and I could go on this trip, and I appreciate your sacrifices. You are a joy in my life, and that's a truth you should never forget. I love you all.

Finally, I thank God for His gifts and His opportunities. He never stopped pursuing me, even when I was running away from Him. I have seen the thread of His purpose throughout my life, and I am thankful for all He has given me.

Table of Contents

Foreword

Choosing to give is a sign of love. Most times, whoever gives expects to be loved back or at least hopes for a pay back of some kind or to receive appreciation from the recipient. It takes unconditional love to do what the missionaries do; sacrificing and taking risks in the name of serving others for the glory of God. You do this for people you would never even see again; who would not ever pay you back or help you in turn, not even recognizing you. This is what Jesus taught us in Mark 5 when he healed a man and the man wanted to hang around and even go with Jesus, but Jesus told him to go and tell others what God had done for him.

This Bless Back medical outreach was one of its kind. They demonstrated what we call service above-self; persevering and enduring all unfavorable circumstances. By the time they arrived, they were already exhausted from the long journey of almost twenty-four hours of travel and connections from plane to plane. I was amazed to see what was accomplished; they used every bit of energy they had and tolerated the few hours of uncomfortable rest every night. It was total service and love shared in this hurting world we live in today.

Thanks to my friend and brother in Christ, Paul, for choosing to capture these stories. This book will help guide those wishing to reach out to the body of Christ, especially in Africa.

Paul, Stephanie and the entire team have embraced God's call upon their lives and they are continuing to be a blessing in any way possible. They use the skills and professionalism they have learnt to offer free service to others and, above all, to share the Good News of Jesus Christ. There is nothing more rewarding and

self-satisfying in life like going out of your way to make another person's life better!

Robert Katende
Sports Outreach
Founder/Director, SOM Chess Academy
(Home of the Queen of Katwe Project)
Transforming Lives Through Chess One move at a Time
http://www.sportsoutreach.net/

African sunset from the plane

Chapter 1

Chasing a Dream

Don't ask yourself what the world needs. Ask yourself
what makes you come alive. And then go do that. Because
what the world needs is people who have come alive.

- Howard Thurman

"Whoa."

I stared at the monitor in the seat in front of me. The map
displaying our flight path showed that we had crossed the
Mediterranean Sea and were now over Egypt. The familiarity of
what I saw made me gasp. My skin tingled as I stared at the tiny
screen in front of me.

Growing up, I attended church with my family every Sunday.
Every time the doors were open, we were there. I had to dress up in
a collared shirt and tie, and I dragged my Bible along every week.
In those days, Bibles were large, leather-bound tomes in the King
James Version. When the sermon turned dull, I opened my Bible
to the maps in the back. I stayed awake by tracing the path Paul
had taken as he brought the gospel into Turkey, Greece, and Italy.
Another chart showed where Jesus went in Israel. The first map
always indicated the path the Israelites took when they left Egypt
during the Exodus. It was this page that blazed across my mind
in the airplane. I was flying over the land reflected on that map.

I saw the Red Sea, where the Israelites escaped pursuit from the Egyptians. I saw the Sinai Peninsula, where Moses received the Ten Commandments. And I saw Egypt and the Nile River, where Joseph rose to power, where Moses was born, and where another Joseph took Jesus to escape Herod. In America, our stories only go back a couple hundred years. I was flying over a place with thousands of years of history. These stories have weight. This land has history.

I looked out the window for a glimpse of this ancient place. Miles below, sand the color of a sugar cookie stretched to the horizon. My wife sat beside me, and I poked her with my elbow. "Stephanie, look. It's our first African sunset." The sun blazed fiery orange and brilliant yellow, making the western horizon appear aflame. I prayed for the fire of God's spirit to flow through our team as we shared His love with the people of Uganda.

My heart pounded, and Stephanie squeezed my hand as I pressed my face to the glass. I couldn't believe this trip was really happening. Words stuck in my throat as I considered everything it had taken to make this mission trip possible.

Less than eight years ago, I had walked away from God, church, and my first wife. My life was a dark emotional blur as we fought over custody of our three children. My bills and debts soared. Like a rusted old boat beached and full of holes, I was a wreck.

As time went by, I created a new home with my children, and things began to stabilize. I still avoided church, feeling like a huge disappointment to God, to my family, and to my children. Since I had grown up with the church, my divorce hit my parents and brother like a spiritual nuclear bomb. As challenging as it was for them, they continued to love me as I went through this difficult time.

Another big part of my newfound stabilization was Stephanie. We were both nurses and worked together at the hospital. God sent her into my life to help me get through some of my darkest days, and we were married in 2010. My parents and brother attended our wedding, and it seemed as if life was headed in the right direction.

Less than a year later, my boss "suggested" I find another job. Once again, the struggle was on as I could only scrape enough money each month to pay the bills. I felt lost. There must be more to life than this.

In July 2012, I found myself returning to church. It felt different from the years of church attendance in my youth. As we were singing, I heard God tell me, "I'm so glad you're home." My faith growing up had been all about religious rules and restrictions. In that moment, my relationship with Jesus became real, and my life has never been the same.

I could fill another book with stories of God's work in my life. He intervened in my work and financial situations in miraculous ways. By the time we left for Uganda, I was becoming a better husband, father, son, and brother. New relationships developed when I started volunteering and leading a men's group at church. In only a few months, God was restoring my heart and answering prayers I didn't even know I had made. I was eager to see Him do more in my life. I wanted to use my gifts in service to Him.

When my friend Bishop asked me to join him on a medical mission to Uganda, I agreed before he even finished asking the question. A smile spread across my face at the thought of using my nursing skills in service to God. But I couldn't go without Stephanie, so I posed the question to her. She paused. Although the love of Jesus had transformed my life, we did not share the same set of beliefs. She saw Christianity as helpful for people who needed it, but she did not surrender to it. Her eyes glowed at the prospect of going to Uganda, but she was uncomfortable with the religious overtones. She didn't want to tell other people what they should or should not believe.

In spite of her concerns, she agreed to go hear more at a meeting at Bishop's house. She said, "I just want the details. I'm not saying yes." I gave her a kiss on the cheek, my heart warm with the prospect of our trip. I asked friends to pray for God to fill her heart with desire to go to Uganda.

Bishop presented general information about Uganda and what we would be doing: six medical clinics—three in the slums of Kampala and three in war-torn northern Uganda—and a safari at the end at Paraa Safari Lodge. My heart beat faster as we saw pictures of the villages and slums where we would be working. I gave Stephanie an encouraging smile and sat on the edge of my seat as the moment of decision neared.

We shared the reasons behind our interest in the trip. After I voiced my desire to utilize my nursing skills, it was Stephanie's turn. My jaw dropped as she spoke. As a little girl, she dreamed of becoming a nurse so that she could take care of people in Africa. Her life had turned in a different direction, and she was unable to take her talents across the ocean. With a clenched jaw, I grabbed her hand, determined to do whatever it took to make her desire come to pass.

Her dream, like many of our dreams, died during the twists and turns of life. She had smothered it, assuming it was hopeless. Killing her dream was better than dealing with the disappointment of being denied.

What dreams have you given up? Do you go through life disengaged, isolated, and bored? It seems easier to go through life without a dream than to experience the pain of having our desires thwarted. But is it really?

Our trip was coordinated with Sports Outreach Institute, a ministry committed to restoring hope and transforming lives. *The Queen of Katwe,* by Tim Crothers, relates the work of this ministry in Kampala. More specifically, it tells how God used

Robert Katende, who worked with Sports Outreach, to change the life of Phiona Mutesi, a girl from the slum of Katwe. Robert coached soccer to children from the slums and gave them a bowl of porridge after practice. He saw many children didn't participate in soccer, so he began teaching chess to these children. Phiona sat through the lesson for the porridge but soon discovered a great talent for chess. As the children's chess skills developed, Robert entered them in local tournaments, where they surprised everyone with excellent performances. Slum kids didn't play chess, much less win at it. With each tournament, these pioneers kept improving, especially Phiona. She became the woman's chess champion for all of Uganda and has played in tournaments throughout the world.

It is an amazing story of the impact one person can make. Disney has made a movie about Phiona's story, and she will be famous. Instead of leaving Kampala and the slums behind, Phiona and Robert have used this movie to help the people in Katwe and expand the ministry of Sports Outreach.

Robert did not grow up with a dream of coaching the chess champion of Uganda. He was a talented soccer player until a traumatic injury turned his life around. Later, as he looked for stable employment, he started working with Sports Outreach and wanted to develop relationships with children in the slums of Kampala. He did not gripe about what he did not have or give up, because opportunity looked different from what he had anticipated. He followed the new dream God gave him, step by step.

Phiona had no intention of having a movie made about her life. She just wanted a bowl of porridge. She wanted to learn this new game she saw other children playing. God used her gift to provide a way for her family to escape the slum, and now she works to help other children find a better life. All because a man dropped a chessboard into the dust of Uganda and began teaching a new game to a bunch of hungry kids.

God has a way of doing amazing things when we take a step in His direction. My problem is I want to see the whole route before I take my first step. I wish God would give me a GPS with turn-by-turn directions so I know what I'm getting into before I commit. I would know where the traffic jams are and how much farther to the next rest stop. A GPS would make following God so much easier.

God doesn't work that way. Psalm 119:105 says, "Your word is a lamp to my feet and a light to my path." God gives us a lamp, not a map. He shows us the next step, not the whole route. If we want to see farther down the road, we have to take another step. And another. And another. Soon we find ourselves in uncharted territory, a place more amazing than anything we would have asked for or imagined.

So, how do we get started? Howard Thurman said, "Ask what makes you come alive and go do that." Psalm 37:4 (NIV) says, "Take delight in the Lord, and He will give you the desires of your heart." And in Proverbs 4:23 (NIV), "Above all else, guard your heart, for everything you do flows from it."

What are your dreams? What does your heart desire? In many cases, life destroys our dreams. Disappointment, hurt, resentment, duties, and responsibilities leave them dying by the side of the road. Do you feel suffocated by the pressure of expectation and the need to perform? Or maybe you're bored with life, and wonder where the meaning is. You go to work, come home, watch TV, and go to bed. Yawn. Every day is the same. Empty. Routine. Insignificant. Is this all there is? Our hearts know better.

We manufacture meaning in our lives the best we can. It can come in the form of video games or fantasy football. We find our meaning in making another sale, another deal at work. We can even pour our lives into volunteering, thinking we will have an impact if we just keep doing and performing. We push to prove our lives have meaning. We need to matter.

Take a minute and ask yourself, "What makes your heart come alive?" I bet it's not a collection of to-do lists and tasks to be checked off. Pray for God to show you the dreams you have locked away. It might be something you suffocated long ago, when life and duty made it seem impossible. You may think you killed it, but there is hope.

Stephanie discovered her dream could be revived. It breathed once more that night in Bishop's living room when she allowed herself to desire again. Your dreams can live again too. We have a God of restoration and resurrection. He breathes new life into dead situations.

But dreaming ain't easy. We have an enemy who tries to distract and disrupt us from pursuing the dreams God gave. He does not want us to walk on God's path. He wants to keep you away from the lamp that lights the way. As we followed our call and prepared to go to Uganda, we discovered this resistance at every turn.

Andrew at the circus

Chapter 2

Dreaming Ain't Easy

Turning your back on the roar will feel good for the
moment . . . But hiding in the thicket, far from the sound
of the wild calling you are meant to pursue, is a far more
sinister opponent you didn't even know was there: death.
The death of the dreams God planted deep down inside
you. The death of the life you were born to live.

- Levi Lusko, *Through the Eyes of a Lion*

Stephanie screamed into the phone. "I can't do it. I'm not
going."

She had just left the passport office without the document she
needed to get to Africa. I could almost hear her heart breaking.
Her dream was dead.

Stephanie despises dealing with bureaucratic inefficiencies.
We were married four years before she changed her name to
McDonald. She loved me, but hated the DMV. The thought of
enduring more administrative hoops gave her palpitations.

She first called me on her way to the passport office. As soon
as I answered, she was yelling into the phone. "These stupid
directions aren't right. Who would put a passport office in the
middle of a warehouse district? I can't find this place, and I've
got things to do!"

I had no idea what was going on, but took a deep breath. She
gave me the address, and I opened up Google to help guide her to
her destination. She continued shouting. "I'm bailing. This whole

idea was stupid. You don't know how much I had to go through just to change my name in the first place. Now this! Men!"

Biting back a scathing response, I prayed for guidance and peace as I directed her to the correct entrance for the office. Stephanie arrived with time to spare. Breathing a sigh of relief, I said, "I love you. Call me when you're finished."

Once inside the office, Stephanie gave the government employee her paperwork, tapping her foot and glancing at her watch while he reviewed it. Looking up, he told her the paperwork was incomplete and she would have to come back later. She responded by screaming about how stupid and ridiculous this whole process was. Her face red and veins popping, she stormed out of the office. I was unprepared for the voice on the phone when she called a few minutes later.

"This is so stupid! I don't have time to waste. I can't do this. I'm not going. You're just going to have to go without me!"

Through her tears, she told me what happened. I interpreted those events to mean she was facing a spiritual attack, something coming against her to prevent her from going to Uganda. Praying for protection, I made a plan. Stephanie was not going to be stopped from going to Africa because of problems with her paperwork. I told her to let me handle it. I would complete the paperwork, schedule the appointment, even drive her to the office. All she had to do was show up.

Over the next several weeks, I continued to reassure Stephanie, confident in the direction we were going. Everyone I knew was praying for the process to be completed without a problem. God gave me a sense of calm as He directed us.

The day arrived. I picked Stephanie up and drove her to the passport office. She kept glancing at me and squeezing her hands together while we waited for her paperwork to be processed. At last we left the office with glowing smiles and light hearts. A few weeks later we held her brand-new passport in our hands. God's protection and provision came through for us, and Stephanie was one step closer to realizing her dream.

You might be asking yourself how I could know it was an enemy attack. You might even ask who this enemy is and why he would care. Satan has been present since the creation of the world, and his entire focus is to disrupt God's plans. The Bible describes him and his tactics. Revelation 12:17 (NIV) reveals the targets of Satan's hatred. "Then the dragon was enraged at the woman and went off to wage war against the rest of her offspring—those who keep God's commands and hold fast their testimony about Jesus." The dragon refers to Satan and the woman is Mary the mother of Jesus. We, Christians, are the rest of her offspring.

Our souls belong to God once we decide to follow Jesus. Satan knows he can't kill us, so he tries to disrupt our relationship with God the Father and limit our effectiveness here on earth. Job lost his children and all his possessions, all in an attempt to make him curse God (Job 1:11, 2:5). Satan goes about as a roaring lion, seeking someone to devour (1 Peter 5:8). His weapons are lies, condemnation, and accusation intended to wound the heart of the believer.

I now expect to be attacked when I am doing something important. If I have a special time of worship or a meaningful event with the family planned, I know things will go awry, emotions will flare out of control, all in an effort to distract and isolate me from God's direction. Let me give you a recent example.

My son Andrew and I were going to see the circus as a special father-son event when he was nine. With three other children, one-on-one time is a special opportunity. I woke up singing to myself, picturing the good times ahead.

We started our morning playing video games until it was time for breakfast. We went to the kitchen to make chocolate-chip pancakes and that's when I discovered Andrew had lied to me.

Without divulging the details, my mood changed in less than a second. Standing over him with my face red and eyes bulging, I yelled about trust and disappointment. Tears welled in his eyes as he stood there listening to my rant. He ran to his room as I took away his toys, his iPod, his chocolate-chip pancakes. I wanted to keep him from playing in his basketball game and going to the circus. I was a bear ready to lash out at anyone in my path. I snapped at my wife and other children, yelling at them just for looking at me. In the midst of this, I knew I was acting like a beast. The spiral continued as I believed the voice in my head. "You're not just acting like a horrible father. You are a horrible father."

Trapped by the condemnation in my mind, I drove to Andrew's game. The car was silent as everyone either looked down or out the window. I realized what was happening. My emotions had flown out of proportion to the reality of the situation. Sure, Andrew had lied to me, but why did I react so strongly? The enemy wanted to destroy my time with Andrew and contaminate our relationship. Tears filled my eyes as I thought of how I hurt my son by allowing the enemy to flood my emotions.

When we parked at the gym, I turned around and apologized to my family and asked for their forgiveness. They lifted their heads as I admitted my sin. Smiles returned to their faces. We walked to the stands with a renewed bond.

Have you experienced something like this? Maybe you ruined a special moment over something you couldn't let go. Or work piled up and you missed out on an important event. Or there was that time your wife said something and you flew into a rage, ruining a wonderful evening. If you could just go back, you would. I hope I'm not the only one who feels like that.

The devil comes to steal, kill and destroy (John 10:10). Can you look back and see areas where he was successful in your life?

Stolen opportunities? Killed dreams? Destroyed relationships? My past is littered with the debris. It is easy to hang our heads with past failures and blame our own weakness and incompetence. You have an enemy who wants to take you out, who initiates events to take away our desire to follow God or derail us from taking a step of faith for the Lord. The devil tries to steal our significance and our dreams through his attacks. And he works with devastating efficiency.

The preparation for our trip to Uganda went well as our departure approached. We packed bags full of medicine, supplies, and soccer equipment. The team met to practice the logistical aspects of the medical clinic. Our friendships grew as we counted down to February 1. Those relationships would be needed as tragedy struck our team only three days before we left. This email described the events that occurred.

"When the alarm went off this morning, few of us realized what this day held in store. We planned on tying up loose ends at work, making final preparations for our trip, spending time with loved ones before we left. Some of us experienced a blocked Providence Road as we tried to get to work. Maybe you awoke to the news of an accident on Providence Road, pictures of a mangled car and advice on different routes to get around the city.

Little did we know that Pam and Hal had been woken up before their alarms by a phone call no parent ever wants to receive. They rushed to the hospital to find their youngest son Stephen broken in so many places. The medics, nurses, policemen, and doctors who took care of him said they don't know how he survived that wreck. His parents had to feel so hurt and angry at the decisions that led to this, and so thankful that he was still alive.

A little after 7 a.m., Bishop sent out a text requesting prayer. Details were sketchy, but we knew there had been an accident. Immediately, our team mobilized to support this family. On a day like today, we weren't a team of people planning to go to Uganda together. We were a family surrounding this family.

The Guices will be unable to accompany us to Uganda. That doesn't seem to matter. We were brought together by more than a desire to go to Africa. We were brought together by a Father who was preparing for this day. To put people in position to respond when their family was attacked, hurt, and in need.

The end is not yet known. Stephen is still in the intensive care unit, requiring high-level monitoring and care to give him the best chance of recovery. He, like every one of us, is in the Father's hands. We pray for His love, His comfort, His healing for Stephen and the Guice family. We will continue to pray for a miraculous healing of Stephen's broken body, and for the Father to send a spirit of peace and comfort over Pam, Hal, and his brother Andrew. Even though they aren't going to Uganda with us, they remain a part of our mission. They remain a part of our team. They will always be our family.

Pam and Hal needed us. The relationships created within our team supported them during this catastrophic event. They weren't familiar with a hospital setting, but our team responded to help alleviate discomfort and minimize the stress in the situation. They were disappointed they would not join us in Uganda, but were thankful God had encircled them with relationships built during the preparation for the mission.

The Guice family became a beacon of strength, peace, and faith during Stephen's hospitalization. Throughout our trip in Uganda, we received updates on Stephen's condition. We celebrated with the Guice family when the doctors removed Stephen's breathing tube. And again when he moved out of the ICU. And once more when he was discharged from the hospital and allowed to go home. Stephen experienced miraculous healing and celebrated his twenty-second birthday in April 2016. Even though Hal and

Pam stayed in Charlotte, we carried them to Uganda in our hearts and in our prayers.

Following Jesus isn't easy. We have an enemy that opposes us. His desire is to devour, steal, kill, and destroy our hopes, dreams, and calling. I could have wounded my son and damaged our relationship. Stephanie wanted to tap out and quit when faced with the challenge of accomplishing her dream. Pam and Hal might have been stuck asking God "Why?" as they sat next to Stephen's hospital bed. The devil wins if we let him. If we forget the second half of John 10:10.

"The thief comes only to steal and kill and destroy. *I came that they may have life and have it abundantly."* (emphasis added). Jesus did not intend for us to live a life of dead dreams and broken relationships. He came to bring us abundant life. A rich life. An overflowing life.

The demons of fear, doubt, and insecurity run rampant in our lives. They rob us of our calling. They destroy our dreams. We hesitate to hope because of the disappointments of the past. I can't imagine the pain and frustration, abuse, and agony you might have been through. Maybe you're in the middle of it right now, and it is impossible to see any light at all. You're at the bottom of the pit, and you have no idea how to get out.

If that is you, I'd like to offer a rope made up of two cords. One cord is John 11:35 (NIV), "Jesus wept." Grief overwhelmed Jesus as he surveyed the scene. One of his best friends, Lazarus, was dead. Lazarus' sisters mourned and wondered where Jesus had been when they needed him. Jesus was about to bring Lazarus back to life and amaze them all. So why did he weep?

Jesus wept to see the effects of sin on those whom he loves. I believe he still does today. He weeps to see us suffer, just as you would if your child was going through a struggle in their life. He is not angry with you. He isn't punishing you. He weeps to see his loved ones hurting. In whatever you are going through right now, He is weeping right there with you.

This weeping is not a hopeless wailing. Jesus was about to raise Lazarus back to life. So we come to the second cord, Romans 8:28 (NIV). "And we know that in all things God works for the good of those who love him, who have been called according to his purpose." Lazarus had to die in order to reveal the miracle of resurrection. Jesus had to die to provide salvation and hope for all those who believe in him. While he weeps beside you, he also knows what is coming next. God is able to take what is meant for evil and turn it for good.

I didn't finish my story about Andrew and the circus. After his game, we were driving to take the train into the city. We had an open conversation about the events of the morning, and I shared my thoughts about the enemy and his impact on our lives. In those moments, what we feel becomes real. I didn't just feel like a horrible father. In my mind, I became a horrible father. We forget the truth that is real, and believe the "truth" that we feel.

Andrew listened and seemed to understand. He was only nine after all. But I wanted him to hear a truth he could hold on to when his feelings were whirling around and he was unsure of reality. I told him, "You are a joy in my life. Even if I don't always act like it, that is always true." His eyes glistened as I had him repeat it back to me. He needs to remember the truth when the lies overwhelm him.

The same is true for us. The Bible is full of truth that is real. Truth we must hold on to when our feelings scream something different. God's word brings light to our dark places.

The knowledge that Satan opposes your life should not discourage you, but should fill you with confidence. When you experience opposition, you know you are doing something important. As the old country preacher says, "If you don't come face to face with the devil, you're probably walking in the same direction." Opposition is a good thing.

We landed in Uganda in the middle of the night. I felt prepared and ready to take on anything the devil could dish out. Our first day of medical clinics revealed a different strategy from the enemy—a subtle attack we endure every day.

Child peeking into the medical clinic
Photo credit: Leigh Ann Loeblein

Chapter 3
I'm Here, But Am I Really?

Many times busyness is often mistakenly equated with
productivity. But those words are not synonymous.
Just because we're spinning our wheels, rushing from
one commitment to the next, doesn't necessarily
mean that we are doing anything worthwhile.

- Crystal Paine

We arrived to a hot, humid environment. The temperature
had been in the mid fifties when we left Charlotte, NC. Here in
Uganda, in the middle of the night it was still in the eighties. The
air in the airport was stale, unmoving, and muggy. I rolled my
pant legs up above my knees as the desire to *be* cool overrode the
desire to *look* cool.

Immigration officials took our temperature, a reminder of the
precautions against the Ebola virus. The outbreak had been a major
concern for many people prior to our departure. The US seemed to
be in a state of panic, convinced that every African carried Ebola,
and many people thought we were headed into the heart of Ebola
country. Uganda was nowhere near the countries with an outbreak,
and we were confident of our safety as we went to the next line.

After getting through customs, the team regrouped at baggage
claim, scrambling to connect to Wi-Fi to let our families know
of our safe arrival. I loaded my cart high with duffle bags and
suitcases, and we stepped out into the Ugandan night.

The parking lot was dark and confusing, and I struggled to keep the bags from falling over. Someone came up out of the dark and asked if I needed help. I had traveled to Jamaica and St. Thomas, and my encounters with the locals were not very positive around the airport. I didn't want to fall victim to allowing someone to help me with my bags only to see them run off with a suitcase full of medical supplies, or charge me $10 to return my suitcase. I responded that I could handle it and continued through the parking lot. We gathered around a bus near the back. My ears grew hot as I realized the offer for help came from our Ugandan partners. The darkness hid my red face as we exchanged greetings. I was eager to load the bags and hide in the van as we drove to our hotel.

My red face turned ashen as soon as we pulled onto the road to Kampala. We were on the wrong side of the road and all I could see was headlights coming toward me. People were everywhere, walking on the side of the road, so close I could have reached out my window and touched them. With no street lights, in almost complete darkness, I thought these people were insane.

We entered Kampala and signs of a more stable infrastructure appeared. Streetlights lined the road, revealing modern buildings. We arrived to the hotel soon after 1 a.m. and unloaded the bags. We grabbed our personal bags to take to our room and shambled off for a short rest; 6:45 would come much too soon.

The first thing we noticed as we entered our room was the mosquito net hanging over the bed. Because of the holes in the net, I was not confident in its mosquito-resisting qualities and was thankful for the permethrin-soaked sleep sacks we brought.

The lack of air conditioning left the room hot and stuffy. We found an old floor fan covered in orange dust and turned it on. The screens outside the window were in better shape than the mosquito netting, so we opened the windows to get cool air circulating through the room.

I headed into the tile-floored bathroom, aware of the warning not to drink the water, even to brush our teeth. Turning on the water, I hoped for some warm water to rinse off hours of travel before going to bed. I let out a nervous laugh and shout of triumph when the water heated up to an acceptable level.

I glanced at Stephanie as I looked at the showerhead, connected to a hose and just lying in the tub. How was this going to work? Our tired minds struggled to figure out a solution until I was hit with inspiration. "Why don't I hold the showerhead and spray you down? After that, you can soap up and I'll rinse the soap off. Then you can return the favor." Stephanie couldn't argue with my logic, but perhaps questioned the mischievous look I was giving her. She accepted my proposal. Not only was it an effective process for cleaning, but it also provided a great opportunity for some romance.

Now clean and somewhat cooled off, we struggled through two layers of mosquito netting and into our sleep sacks. It is important to have everything you need before you climb in. After taking five minutes to get settled, I was aggravated to see my water bottle across the room. I wish I could say it only happened once, but I guess I'm a slow learner. Soon after 2 a.m., I fell into a restless sleep. Between the confining sleep sack, the netting hanging in my face, and the hot, humid environment, I tossed and turned throughout the night in spite of my exhaustion.

A staticky, metallic voice jolted me out of my haze at 5 a.m. Mosques filled Kampala, and the call to prayer resounded throughout the city. I didn't sleep much after that. As the morning sun brought light to a sky colored dusty pink and blue, I stepped out onto the balcony off our room, excited for my first real look at Uganda, the Pearl of Africa. Our room overlooked a courtyard.

Giant birds nested in the trees lining the river off to my right. The vegetation and beauty revealed by the African sunrise felt foreign and surreal.

We went to breakfast and sat outside, braving the early morning mosquitoes to enjoy the cooler air. People shuffled in, bleary eyed, smelling of bug spray and looking for caffeine to help wake up. Our only coffee option was Nescafé instant coffee—a disappointment to many on our team. Ugandan coffee is known for being very good, and we looked forward to drinking it throughout our visit. Because the water wasn't safe, it had to be boiled first, and our only options were tea and instant coffee.

Conversations were muted as the reality of the challenge facing us set in. The anxiety was as palpable as the humidity. We sat in a foreign country, about to do something none of us had ever done before. With wide eyes and nervous hearts, we organized our supplies and loaded the vans for our medical clinic in the slum of Katwe.

Rush hour in Kampala defied sanity. Cars, trucks, and vans overflowed the road. People on motorcycles—boda-bodas—weaved in and out between the larger vehicles. The boda-bodas were a major mode of transportation in Uganda. Although they were the cheapest, they were not very safe. Traffic laws appeared nonexistent in the pandemonium.

People were everywhere, walking down the road, through traffic, sitting by bunches of bananas or walking with jerry cans on their heads. Most of the people in Kampala live at least thirty minutes from the closest source of water, and they use the yellow plastic cans to carry it home. As we rode down the road, my head was on a swivel, trying to absorb everything I saw, heard, and smelled.

It was difficult to process. On one hand, I had started the day just like any other day. I had eaten breakfast, gotten dressed and was now on the way to work. On the other hand, it was very clear I was no longer in the US. Bananas and sides of beef hung from the roof of a shack beside the dusty road. Rusted out and dented vans rested on top of shops. People sold eggs from what looked to be a storage unit, but was in fact the concrete floor where they had slept the previous night. New construction was held up by branches no thicker than my arm. My brain struggled to handle it all.

We pulled off the main road, turning into an open space between two buildings. Winding our way through the shanties, the bus stopped in front of a ramshackle blue building. With tears in his eyes and his voice shaking, Bishop reminded us of our impact. "You have the chance to touch one life. Don't let the opportunity pass." After a short prayer, we piled off the bus to set up for the clinic. We crossed a bridge over a four-foot ditch next to the road. I looked down and gagged as I realized the ditch served as the sewer system. Rendered speechless and lightheaded by what I saw and smelled, I joined the team inside.

Building codes don't exist in Katwe. The warped planks left large gaps where children peeked through. Limbs held the structure together. No lumber, no two-by-fours, just branches. Bare bulbs dangled from the supports, providing a flickering light. Curtains hung from clotheslines to create small rooms where the providers would see the patients. In the corners of the building, more light came through the cracks in the walls than from the lightbulbs overhead.

We gathered with the team of Ugandan volunteers from Sports Outreach. I saw Robert and Phiona across the circle as Dr. Barungi, our team medical director from Uganda, gave instructions. Pointing to the different areas, she said, "Triage is here, then the patient goes there to see a provider. If they need lab work, they go to this door, and this table will be our pharmacy."

The team jumped into action organizing medications and creating triage stations. Through the back door, I saw patients waiting in hard plastic chairs under a white canopy. In each clinic, people sat for hours in the queue, never trying to cut, never complaining, just waiting.

The opening minutes of the clinic reminded me of going to the symphony. When the orchestra first shows up and tunes their instruments, everything is chaotic and discordant. The players are each doing their own thing. They align their instruments to a consistent note and the melodies blend together until the conductor taps his baton on the stand. Silence, and then beautiful music explodes.

As patients trickled in through registration, our team was out of sync, running into each other. Three people did one job, and nobody did another. Stephanie settled into triage and welcomed every person she saw with a warm smile. If they brought a child, her eyes brightened and she held out her hands to hold them. She had a glow about her as she cared for these people, many of whom couldn't understand a word she said. What they could understand was the warmth in her eyes, the smile she gave them, the caring in her touch.

After triage, the providers, made up of doctors, nurse practitioners, physician assistants, and medical students, would see the patients in their cloth cubicles. At least three people squeezed into these tiny spaces: the provider, the patient, and an interpreter.

Our interpreters were vital parts of our team. They helped communicate questions about health conditions from the providers and answers from the patients. Once the initial conversation was over, the interpreters took charge. They asked the patient if they would like someone to pray with them and almost all of them did. The volunteers shared about Jesus and asked if the patient would like to know more. These conversations occurred while the provider was writing down the orders for lab or pharmacy. The provider would hand the prescription to the interpreter, who would inform them, "This one is ready to accept Jesus, and they want us to pray with them." This marriage of spiritual and medical practice is a radical departure from the process in the US and took some getting used to.

While we wanted to provide medical care to people in need, our primary purpose was to share the love of Jesus. The medical clinic was the delivery tool. Many people we saw had never experienced love in any form. We decided to provide the care first, and let them know the "why" afterward. This approach challenged our western way of thinking. We tend to see people waiting as a captive audience to hear the gospel. We didn't want our patients to feel as if they needed to say they believed our message in order to receive care.

Jesus used this same process during His ministry. He healed people first. He saw their needs and had compassion on them. We simply followed His model.

As the day warmed up, the clinic overflowed with people, talking, and laughter. The orchestra played beautiful music, in sync and in tune as we worked to see our patients. Without warning, our workspace darkened. The providers in the corners didn't even have enough light to read the charts. Outside, wind kicked up dust and sent trash through the houses like tumbleweeds. Dark clouds rolled in. We stared as the skies opened up and the rain began to pour down.

Rain in Katwe causes problems. The slum is located on a flood plain, and the torrential rain submerges homes. Stories in *The Queen of Katwe* describe times when mothers returned home to drowned children who could not escape the rising waters. We experienced a taste of the rainy season and the horror it can bring.

Remember the ditch? The water flowing across the floor

included more than water and dirt. Raw sewage spilled over the ditches and across the ground, smelling awful and contaminating everything it touched.

We ran to rescue our medical supplies. We used benches, chairs, and tables to keep the equipment safe from the cocoa-colored fluid running over the floor. Patients crowded into the building to get out of the rain; they were soon packed shoulder to shoulder. Electricity failed, and the lights went out. Trapped in the dark, sweat dripping off our faces, we did the only thing we could do. We started singing.

Do you find yourself trapped? Are you unhappy at work, stuck in a job you don't want to do? Have you been betrayed by a friend who shifted the blame of failure onto you? Maybe your high-school-aged daughter told you she's pregnant. Do you look across the table at a wife you feel you don't know anymore? Life can feel like prison, and the chains can take many forms.

The apostle Paul knew about prison. In Acts 16, he found himself in a jail cell, going nowhere in the middle of the night. If I was in his situation, I imagine I would respond something like this: Rubbing my ankles raw trying to escape the chains. Screaming at God, "Why am I in here?" Lying down with a sigh, resigned to my fate. I don't handle imprisonment well.

But how did Paul respond? By praying and singing hymns to God. And then the door to the prison blew open.

I'm learning to change my reaction, although I prefer for the jail cell to open and the chains to come off first. What's there to sing about while I'm in lockdown? For some inspiration, it helps to look to the Psalms.

David found himself in some pretty bad situations. He was chased by Saul as a renegade on the run for his life. His own son led a rebellion to take the throne. David had an affair, killed the woman's husband and had a baby with her. And David was "a man after God's own heart."

The Psalms reflect David's struggles. You can read how he dealt with frustration, loneliness, betrayal, and devastation. In the midst of his darkness, he still found a way to praise God. David's singing opened the doors to his prisons.

God wants to break the bars to your prison. The situation may not change—same job, same daughter, same wife. It is your heart God wants to set free. The purpose in redemption is to heal the brokenhearted and open the prison for those who are bound (Isaiah 61:1). As David and Paul discovered, freedom is found by singing and focusing on God more than on your circumstances. Freedom is forgiveness for your friend. Loving your daughter in her struggle. Seeing your wife with new eyes and a fresh heart. That is true freedom, and it can be found in any inescapable situation.

As we sang, the rain stopped and the sun came out. The floor glistened with water and excrement. Our supplies were scattered throughout the clinic. We needed to reset the clinic and get ready to see patients again. But how?

The Ugandan volunteers pulled buckets and sponges out of nowhere, soaking up the brown water from the floor and squeezing it out into the buckets. Robert and Phiona worked side by side with the team. I watched them, speechless, as these two people squeezed the gut-wrenching contents from the floor. They displayed the love and compassion they have for the people in the slums. They do everything they can to help them. It was unforgettable.

Thanks to their work and the warmth of the sun, the floor was dry and we were ready to see patients in minutes. I settled in to help with triage, moving patients back to the providers as quickly as possible. The sun had returned and it looked like everyone in Katwe had come to see us. We wanted to see them all.

Looking back, triage was a blur. I made funny faces for the children and wanted the patients to feel welcome, but the line of people stretched out the door and around the corner. All I really cared about was moving patients through triage faster. The more we saw, the better. Volume was my goal; speed, my focus.

I do remember one man from the chaos of that first day. He had injured his leg a week before, and now the wound appeared swollen and infected. The odor from the wound made more than one person gag. The provider performed the procedure necessary to clean out his infection and bandaged his wound. We gave him an antibiotic to continue the healing process. If he had waited one more week to see a doctor, the infection would have cost him his leg.

An amputation is a death sentence in Uganda. He would be unable to work or keep his wound clean. He couldn't afford the necessary care or medicine and he would have died soon after. His outcome changed because we were there to do a simple procedure and give him medicine. He is still alive because we were there.

The rest of the day was a whirl of people, dust, and smells. Soon we packed up to return to our hotel. We exchanged high fives and fist bumps when Dr. Barungi announced we saw 255 patients. We made an impact and changed lives and loaded the bus ready to recharge and do it again the next day.

As we traveled back to the hotel, several people fell asleep, leaving me alone with my thoughts. I began to feel uneasy as I replayed the day in my mind. In triage, I felt like I was in a competition to move the most patients through. I was frustrated at the things I didn't get to do. I watched other people who made a difference and had long conversations with each other. Kim and Reuben played with kids as they sang and laughed. I had been stuck in triage, with no time to make a connection with anyone. I figured Kim and Reuben brought more joy in ten minutes than I did all day long. I wanted to play with the kids, to get to know someone, to have an impact. I felt empty and disconnected. Sighing and running my hands through my hair, my heart sank as I considered my day wasted.

So many times, chasing the completion of a task gets us in trouble. We puff out our chest, a sense of accomplishment prevailing over everything else. "Look at all I got done today." In the evening, alone with our thoughts, we know something is missing. The check list might be completed, but where was the connection? Where is the meaning?

I struggled with my frustration and wrote in my journal: *Father, help me build relationships. Help me identify the true need, what You have in mind to show them. I want to be part of a powerful event, of a life change. And when I am, help me to see it and recognize it, and not just to dismiss it. Thank you, Father, for this opportunity. Help me to take full advantage of it.* I had no idea how quickly God would answer my prayer.

Girl at peace
Photo credit: Leigh Ann Loeblein

Chapter 4

God Responds

We can only belong when we offer our most authentic
selves and when we're embraced for who we are.

- Brené Brown, *The Gifts of Imperfection*

After a restful night, we drove to the slum of Nateete. The
bus squeezed between the small brick shanties crowding each
other and the road. People sold eggs, milk, and bananas, sitting
on the ground with their wares. As we drove by, I looked inside
the run-down buildings. Mats and clothes were scattered across
the concrete slabs, cramped spaces enough for only one or two
people to lie down. The morning would come and the sleepers
became sellers, tossing their few possession to the side as they tried
to make enough money to survive another day.

Nateete was a different world from Katwe. Lush green grass
spread in front of the church. Cows with huge horns ambled
past to drink from the nearby well. On top of the verdant hill
was a shining white church, standing apart from the small dark
buildings surrounding it. The glass windows gave the building a
light and open feel, and a gentle breeze refreshed us as we unloaded
the bus. Spacious and bright, the church in Nateete seemed like a
mansion compared to the dark, cramped space in Katwe.

I set my goal for the day with calm and focus. I would not repeat my mistakes from yesterday. I focused on working with purpose. The temptation to be task oriented tugged at me during the setup, but I followed Reuben out of the church to see what he would do.

The second I walked out of the door, a little boy bounded up the steps and grabbed my hand. I sat down with him and found myself swarmed by curious little children. They chattered and tried to communicate with me, but the only word I understood was "mzungu," the Lugandan term for "white people." The word references the missionaries who once wandered the country, traveling from village to village to spread the gospel. Mzungu specifically means "one who wanders without purpose." The word stuck for all white people in Kampala.

The children were eager to grab my attention. If I looked away for too long, they would pull my arm or my shirt to turn my eyes back toward them. As the crowd of patients grew, our group blocked the steps and we had to move. The children dragged me by my hand onto the grass where we sat on some old tires. Bishop's presence across the yard grabbed their attention, and they amused themselves running back and forth between us. With mischief lighting up his eyes, Bishop knelt down and whispered something to the children. From the animated way Bishop acted and the giggles that erupted from the children, I prepared for shenanigans. Bishop yelled, "Go!" and laughing children rushed toward me, knocking me off the tire and into the grass. Bishop introduced the term "tickle" to these eager students, and they wanted to implement their new-found knowledge on an unknowing victim. Bishop strutted nearby, taking pictures of his successful maneuver. We sat gasping for breath a few minutes later when I was called to help in triage. I waved goodbye to my new little friends and went to work.

Wet and itchy from the dewy grass, I went to triage with a happy glow. My time with the children refreshed me as the morning heated up. The light breeze from earlier disappeared as patient after patient moved through the clinic.

When I took a break later, I discovered my cohort of children had grown. They crowded around me as soon as I exited the church. I used my stethoscope to listen to their hearts. As I heard their hearts in my ears, I made a noise of what it sounded like. "Dub-dub." I let them hear, putting the earpieces into their ears and holding the bell to my chest. Their eyes widened, and smiles broke across their faces as they heard my heartbeat. They cried out, "This one! This one!" They all wanted their turn listening to the mzungu's heart. Other children flocked to us, attracted by something new. After a time that was much too short, I returned to triage.

I enjoyed this day much more because I focused on being intentional in my actions and less driven to complete tasks. The siren song of the to-do list is seductive. Something about checking off an item feels so good in that moment. When we think about what we've done at the end of the day, we might have a list with everything crossed off, but what impact did we have? Did we interact with anyone in a meaningful way?

I get anxious when my yard looks bad (which is most of the time). The flower beds are full of weeds; the grass needs to be mowed and edged. I worry about how it looks and get frustrated when I don't have enough time to take care of it. I put so much stress on myself to get things done. But why?

What eternal goal will be accomplished if I have a well-manicured lawn? So many things we try to get done just don't matter from a heavenly perspective. I keep reminding myself of a saying I heard about balance. "On their deathbed, no one ever says I wish I spent more time at work." Or doing yard work. Ask yourself, what has value to you? Where can you find your meaning? What will you regret on your deathbed? You still have time to redirect your energy. Find what matters. Spend time doing it. Let go of expectations and demands of others to do what God called you to do.

Stephanie and I sat in the bus later that day eating lunch when a car skidded to a stop in front of the church. A man jumped out asking for a doctor. A girl in the back seat appeared to be having some sort of seizure or asthma attack. Stephanie and a few others carried her inside and placed her on one of the couches. People surrounded her. Some prayed for the girl with hands on her shoulders and head, their eyes squeezed shut with effort and focus. Other team members assessed the situation from a medical standpoint. Stephanie listened to the girl's breathing and heard air moving, which ruled out asthma. Our providers did not believe it was a true seizure. The girl received a shot and her activity decreased to the point she could respond to our questions. I asked the provider what she gave the patient. I thought it was valium. The provider leaned over and whispered, "Nothing. It was just saline." The girl rested with her hands folded over her stomach. Her eyes were alert, and her breathing was slowed. The crisis was averted, but the strangeness was not over.

Reuben had watched from across the room. He was a non-medical person and wanted to stay out of the way during the emergency. As people wandered back to other patients, he made eye contact with the girl and decided to pray over her. As he prayed, her calm demeanor gave way to coughing, choking, and spitting. She convulsed like she was going to throw up, and then went limp. She opened her eyes and looked up at Reuben and Steve, another member of our team who had walked over. She gave them an angelic, peaceful smile and closed her eyes, drifting off to sleep. Steve's stomach lurched and his face went pale. He asked Reuben, "What just happened in there?"

Reuben's response, his voice shaking and tremulous, wasn't exactly reassuring. "I think we just saw a demonic presence come out of her." Shaken by what they had seen, they spent some time outside, praying and processing what happened.

Later in the day, I saw the girl as she spoke with Bishop. She put her trust in Jesus and carried a Bible in her hand. With bright eyes and a gentle smile, she exuded peace and calm. Whatever plagued her before was gone. The transformation was startling.

I am sure this sounds crazy to you. A girl with a demon? You might be saying, "That stuff doesn't happen anymore." I would argue that way of thinking hides it from view. When faced with hard-hearted disbelief in Mark 6 (also paralleled in Matthew 13), Jesus limited his miracles. His power was not lessened, but He chose not to force Himself upon people who lacked faith. Where faith is small, the miracles are miniscule. When faith is great, the miracles are amazing.

More than 450 patients received care at our clinic in Nateete. The last one I saw stands out most. I was sitting on the stage of the church and playing peek-a-boo with a little girl named Hope. One of our providers asked if anyone was available to pray with her patient. I jumped at the chance to participate in a salvation experience. I went with Brittany, a nurse from our team, and a pastor from Uganda named Aloysius to talk with her. Aloysius asked what brought her to the clinic. Although I won't share the specifics of her particular story, the themes of her situation are found throughout the slums.

Women in Uganda lead difficult lives. The culture teaches and encourages them to become dependent on men for their well-being. Many women run off with the first man to get them pregnant, believing they have achieved financial security. The slums are littered with women who have been left in the lurch by a man who disappeared, died, or ran off with another woman.

After the abandonment, women find themselves strapped with caring for a child, searching for lodging and employment, only to find both in short supply. Many women try to find stability through the arms of another man, but this stopgap approach doesn't work for long. The new men don't want to be responsible for raising someone else's child. The women scratch out a meager existence in Kampala, but never seem to find security. No matter how hard they try, escape from this cycle seems impossible.

This particular woman traveled across town to see us in Nateete. Although she considered herself Muslim, something about Christians drew her in. The peace she saw in us evaded her. We were different, and she wanted what we had.

Aloysius explained what trusting in Jesus meant, and he asked Brittany and me if we wanted to say anything. Looking in her eyes as he interpreted, I told the woman, "We all owe a great debt to God and find ourselves unable to pay. Jesus came to eliminate our debts and reunite us with God. And when Jesus chooses us, no one can keep us away. He promised never to leave us, or forsake us."

She told us she wanted to believe in Jesus, and Aloysius led her in her first prayer. She admitted being a sinner, with no hope of getting to God on her own. She put her trust in Jesus as her hope of salvation and reconciliation with God. In Acts 16, the guard asked the apostle Paul, "What must I do to be saved?" Paul's response was to "believe on the Lord Jesus Christ, and you shall be saved." The woman in Nateete verbalized her new belief and claimed a new heart.

Brittany prayed with her next and praised God for being a God of love, praised Him for loving this woman enough to bring a team of Americans around the world to share Jesus with her. After Brittany, I prayed, "Heaven rejoices with the return of one lost sheep, and now heaven is rejoicing over her. I am so thankful to have our debts paid by you, Jesus. Thank you for allowing us to share in her transformation."

Our clinic closed for the day and we loaded the bus to head back to the hotel. The sun was setting in Kampala as the children lined the roads, waving goodbye and running with the bus until they could no longer keep up. Even though we saw so many people, I looked over the houses representing so many more in need. Tears filled my eyes as we left Nateete, my heart full of love for them.

As we traveled along the dusty road, I thanked God for the experiences He gave me. I replayed the scenes from the day and prayed I would not forget them. Each one was an answered prayer from my Father. Playing and interacting with the children. Being part of someone's salvation. My heart overflowed with thankfulness for the gifts my Father had given me.

Bishop and Kristy at Koro Farm

Chapter 5

"This Is Amazing!"

A dream doesn't become reality through magic; it
takes sweat, determination and hard work.

- Colin Powell

The next morning we drove to the site of the new Sports
Outreach ministry center. We assumed the role of sightseers,
filling the bus with laughter and chatter as we made our way
through Kampala. The bus bounced in the potholes of the road
through the slums as we listened to music. "How He Loves" by
the David Crowder*Band played through the speakers.

How He Loves
David Crowder*Band

He is jealous for me,
Loves like a hurricane,
I am a tree,
Bending beneath the weight of His wind and mercy.
When all of a sudden,
I am unaware of these afflictions eclipsed by glory,

And I realize how beautiful You are,
And how great Your affections are for me.

(Chorus) And oh, how He loves us, oh
Oh, how He loves us,
How He loves us all

(Bridge) And we are His portion and He is our prize,
Drawn to redemption by the grace in His eyes,
If His grace is an ocean, we're all sinking.
And Heaven meets earth like an unforeseen kiss,
And my heart turns violently inside of my chest,
I don't have time to maintain these regrets,
When I think about the way . . .

That He loves us,
Oh, how He loves us
Oh how He loves us,
How He loves us all.

I looked out the window, tears filling my eyes as I prayed this song over every dusty house, each person we passed. My heart broke for the people I saw. Their lives were so difficult. They spent every bit of energy just to survive each day. In the midst of their desperation and poverty, I prayed they could somehow see and experience the love and peace of Jesus. I envisioned the prayers spreading out behind our bus like the wake behind a boat.

One line stands out: "I am unaware of these afflictions eclipsed by glory." These people wouldn't find jobs, food, or clean water because they believed in Jesus. They wouldn't get a house or an easy life. The afflictions would remain. The situation wouldn't change. But their outlook would.

Plenty of people own homes full of nice things but don't have peace. They can't find joy or real love. I've lived an "If only" life. "If only I had that job, I'd be set." "If only I had more time." "If only my kids were older." If only, if only, if only. We keep striving for the thing we think will bring us peace, secure our relationships, and validate us. But we come up short and exhaust ourselves in the pursuit.

The offer of the gospel is more than fire insurance to save us from hell. Jesus came to bring peace, freedom, and healing. While many turn to Jesus to check off the box of forgiveness, they try to find everything else on their own. It's a seductive path to follow.

Maybe you feel trapped in your marriage and try to find freedom through drinking, other relationships, or divorce. You might feel rejected by friends and overlooked at work, so you try to perfect your performance to find acceptance. It's like being trapped in quicksand – the harder you try to escape, the faster you sink. You can't escape. You can't find freedom and peace on your own.

We need Jesus. He came to bring good news to the poor, to give sight to the blind and set the captives free (Luke 4:18). The good news is not, "You will no longer be poor." It is, "You won't be blind or captive anymore." We will see how much our Father loves us. We are set free from sin and death. And when we find the peace, freedom, and healing Jesus came to give, we realize the rest of the stuff doesn't really matter as much. We can find a peace, love, and joy that can't be found in the things of this world. We find heaven here on earth. As I prayed the song playing through the speakers, I wanted the people in Uganda to find heaven through a relationship with Jesus. I wanted them to lose sight of their afflictions and struggles in the glory of His love.

After a few more turns, we left the city and discovered a new side of Uganda. Lush foliage and rolling hills replaced the dust-covered shacks of the slums. We drove through small villages, no more than a few block-shaped houses that doubled as store fronts. The transition was remarkable.

We arrived at the ministry center and tumbled out of the bus, eyes wide open to take in everything. The undulating emerald hills and fields. The buildings already built and the promise of more to come. Many of my friends were overwhelmed with the power of the moment. They had worked with Sports Outreach for many years, and tears came to their eyes as they saw their vision becoming a reality.

When construction is complete, children from the slums will live here. Several members of the Sports Outreach team already host children who have no place to go. Many years ago, Moses saw a young boy waiting around the field after soccer practice. When he asked why the boy didn't go home, he discovered the young man didn't have a home. Moses said it was difficult to talk about the spiritual needs of the children while ignoring their obvious physical necessities. He took it upon himself to address those needs. Many more children from the slums will have a roof over their heads and a safe place to sleep at the ministry center because of the work Sports Outreach is doing.

I walked on the concrete slab that will become a basketball court. I looked over the field where soccer games will be held. The soccer field is especially important for the Good News Soccer Club. The team consists of players from the slums who play matches against other neighborhood and school teams. After the games, the players share the gospel with everyone there. When the field is complete, Sports Outreach will host the Resurrection Week tournament. Over 6,000 people show up to watch the Resurrection Week tournament, held the week before Easter. They come to a soccer tournament, and they are invited to know Jesus. Thousands of people have heard the gospel through this ministry, and this field will allow more people to hear the good news.

We established our clinic in a couple of concrete-block buildings. They felt nice and cool with a breeze blowing through for much of the day. Our location was more remote than in the slums, so people trickled in throughout the morning. I wandered between the buildings, doing whatever odd jobs needed to be done. I kept eyeing the prayer tent, looking for an opportunity to spend time there. I had never shared the gospel before, and my heart pounded at the thought of looking someone in the eye as I told them about Jesus. When Jimmy suggested I take a turn at the prayer tent, my shaking legs somehow carried me to it.

I sat down with Leigh Ann and Juventan, our Ugandan translator, and listened as he told a woman about Jesus. I wanted to watch someone else share first. Juventan used something called an Evangecube to help communicate. Pictures are powerful communication tools in Uganda. The Evangecube looked similar to a Rubik's cube, except instead of colors, the sides made pictures. It opened and rotated to show scenes of the gospel story. When Juventan asked the woman if she wanted to place her faith in Jesus, she said yes. We prayed with her to ask Jesus to give her a new heart. Juventan made it look easy.

After I had prayed with a couple people, a man sat down with us, and I presented the gospel. My voice felt strained and my heart raced as I shared Jesus for the first time with a complete stranger. He listened and asked some thoughtful questions. He said he wanted to learn more before he made a decision. I took a shaky breath as he left, my heart rate returning to normal. God says His Word will not return void, and I pray God will cause the seed I planted to grow and bloom into faith.

Sophie came to the tent and asked us to pray for her abdominal pain. She had been to so many doctors and no one could find a reason behind it. She didn't know what else to do. I asked what she knew about Jesus. She laughed a little and said she was a Muslim and didn't know very much. I explained how we are separated from God because of the things we do, but Jesus came down from heaven to take our place, to take the punishment we deserved. And then He came back to life, and we now have access to God. All we have to do is put our hope in Him. I looked in her dark-brown eyes and asked what she thought. In a quiet, awe-filled voice, she responded, "That is amazing." I laughed and agreed with her. She told me she wanted a new heart, and I led her in a prayer to put her trust in Jesus. She seemed so happy and full of peace afterward as she talked with Juventan about getting connected with the local church.

My mind reeled at the unexpected ease of her conversion. It didn't match what I had seen before. In America, talking about your beliefs is awkward. People who don't go to church think they know a lot about Christianity. They argue and challenge everything with a preset disposition about faith. They don't just sit there with a "wow" on their faces and say, "This is amazing." In all likelihood, an unbelieving American treats you with condescension and disdain, a sneer that says, "You really believe that?"

Many people in Uganda have never heard the story of the gospel before. They didn't display the argumentative attitude I see in the US, and I was unprepared for the simple acceptance of the gospel. I realized it wasn't the medical care, or the cubes, or even my speaking skills that made Jesus so compelling. It was the effective work of the Holy Spirit in their hearts.

The day continued, and morning turned to afternoon. Before we were ready, the time arrived to say goodbye. Many of the Ugandans who worked with us in Kampala would not join us in Gulu. Tears filled everyone's eyes as we exchanged hugs with those we would leave behind. After three short days, our heartfelt tears of farewell were for our close brothers and sisters.

Over those three days, amazing things happened, and we had front row seats. Over nine hundred patients came to our medical clinics. At least eighty people received a new heart through Jesus, their lives forever changed. It is impossible to experience and see what we did and remain unaffected. The work we did impacted these people. They would never be the same, and neither would we.

As we returned to our hotel, I looked at the pictures we took as we prepared for departure. I didn't really recognize the people in the photos. It felt like I was looking at a mask designed to represent someone I knew.

I looked around the bus and didn't see the people from the pictures. During the medical clinics, we shared and exposed our hearts. We connected at a soul level. I now saw the true person, the seed inside the shell. As we continued with our mission, this connection became a lifeline of encouragement and support. Our next few clinics involved taking a message of hope and healing to people in northern Uganda who had been wounded and traumatized. Our message would be opposed, and we would need God and each other to get through the times ahead.

The next morning, I found myself caught up in the hectic preparations for our departure. We loaded the bus and began our trip to Gulu. Our excitement bubbled over as we looked out the windows and tried to soak up the scenery. The chatter never ceased as we made our way north; we were in awe of the changing scenery. Brick buildings and densely populated areas became mud huts and sporadic villages. Rolling green hills morphed into hot, dry expanses of grass.

The bus slowed as we approached the bridge over the Nile River. We disembarked and walked across on foot. The Ugandan officer on duty instructed us we could take pictures from the bridge, but not of it. The bridge is one of the few access points to northern Uganda and would be a high priority military target. Looking at the rifle slung over his shoulder, I had no thoughts of disobeying his instructions.

The Nile River is only rivaled by the Amazon as the longest river in the world. The headwaters are located in Burundi until it feeds into Lake Victoria. From there, the Nile meanders more than 4,000 miles north until it spills into the Mediterranean Sea in Egypt. Almost 100,000 cubic feet *per second* are displaced by the powerful flow. I scanned the scene, absorbing a picture that no camera can capture. Lush green foliage draped over the sides of the river. A leaf dropped into the water and immediately disappeared as it was swept away in the swirling current.

Stepping onto the bridge sent a shock through my body. The surge echoed the feeling I had when I saw the map as we flew over this ancient land. An impression of importance, weight, and history surged through my body. I was staggered by the enormity of this river. I had read about the Nile all my life, in church and in school. To be crossing it now felt significant, and I took as many pictures as I could. It is a miracle no one was run over as traffic flowed around us.

The quality of the road to Gulu shifted after we crossed the Nile. The paved roads with two lanes were gone, replaced by a dirt road with occasional portions of tarmac. Giant holes, washed out during the rainy season, demanded precise driving. Traffic became a terrifying spectacle—the Ugandan version of chicken. Oncoming trucks would fly down the road in our direction, and one of us would yield by veering to the side at the last minute. As we lurched from side to side, avoiding the washouts and other vehicles, one of our guides turned and asked a question out of nowhere. "How do you know when a Ugandan is driving drunk?" Stumped, I shrugged my shoulders and almost fell out of my seat as our driver swerved the bus, missing the oncoming traffic by inches. Grinning, he replied, "It is the car that is driving straight." I chuckled and then grimaced as I bounced out of my seat, receiving my first African massage (their term for a hot, bouncing ride).

The miserable drive was brought about because of the years of war and struggle with Joseph Kony and his Lord's Resistance Army (LRA). The LRA occupied the land north of the Nile for more than twenty years. During this time, maintenance of the roads was impossible. The painful drive north was our first taste of the devastation northern Uganda experienced under Kony and the LRA.

I couldn't wait to get off the bus. I was dusty and sore, and fidgeting to stretch my legs. When we finally arrived, I was thankful our hosts offered a tour of the campus and we followed our guide as he shared the mission of Koro Farm, which is the base of operations for Sports Outreach in northern Uganda. Villagers lack basic knowledge of farming and animal husbandry because the men who had the knowledge were killed during the attacks by the LRA. Sports Outreach uses the property to teach the local villages how to grow crops and raise animals.

We saw crops growing in abundance: mango, bananas, papaya, even okra. Animals roamed through the property. Bishop and Kristy walked hand in hand, trying to take it in. Tears filled their eyes as they spoke of the scarcity they saw in 2012—years before. At that time, the farm consisted of one goat and one cow. They experienced the reality of a vision they had dreamed about and worked toward. We walked through schools for the children, a brand new worship center, and the foundation for the medical clinic. We celebrated what God had done already, and looked forward with excitement and anticipation towards what would come.

Christine's House stood apart from the other buildings on the property. Sexual abuse is an epidemic in northern Uganda, and many girls who suffered abuse were outcast from their homes and villages. They found a safe place for themselves and their children here on Koro Farm. Aloysius and Esther, the directors of the center, cared for these girls and taught them how to care for themselves. Christine's House is a place where the girls can recover from the shame of abuse and understand their identity and beauty in Christ.

The sky faded from pink to a dark purple as our tour ended and we reunited with the team. Bats flew overhead as the Ugandan team in Gulu introduced themselves. By the time Aloysius asked Bishop to introduce the Americans, the sky was completely dark. Bishop laughed. "Sorry, Aloysius, but I can barely see Kristy sitting right next to me. There's no way I could introduce my team in the dark. I'll introduce them in the morning, if that's all right." We closed our time with a prayer and headed to the bus. Aloysius came to Bishop and asked him if it was really too dark for him to see. When Bishop nodded yes, Aloysius eyes widened and he stroked his chin. He and the other Ugandans could see perfectly well in the African night. Just one more example how different we are. Blind as the bats flying overhead, we loaded the bus and headed to our hotel in Gulu.

We arrived at our lodging to find a buffet ready on the patio. Flowers and greenery abounded as we relaxed in the cool night air. When we discovered our rooms had air conditioning and Western-style showers, we wolfed down dinner to rest and get ready for the next day. After spending the day in the heat of the bus, I couldn't wait for a refreshing shower and cool air to sleep in.

As I wrote in my journal trying to capture our day, pictures from the two ministry centers flashed through my mind. The hill overlooking the soccer field. The foundation of the medical clinic. The walls of the chess academy, still under construction.

The fields and animals. And yet, the properties in Kampala and Koro Farm represented so much more than land and buildings.

Years of planning, prayers, and preparation paved the way for the property I walked on that day. The ministry centers started as an idea in someone's mind, a dream with no plans to stand on. But the dream didn't die. The person kept asking, "How can I do this?" over and over until the vision became a reality.

What dreams do you have? You might have killed them on the altar of "reality" in an effort to get your head out of the clouds. But all that did was assassinate a little bit of your heart. Your desires might have been suffocated by the pressures of everyday life. You might think it's too foolish, too "out there," for you to pursue. It's time to get your heart and your dreams back.

Your dreams don't have to be overly ambitious. One of my dreams is to see my children grow and have a relationship with Jesus. I dream of a relationship with my wife where we are unified and aligned in our adventure together. Dreams don't even need to leave the house.

Finding a dream is the easy part. Katherine Paterson said, "A dream without a plan is just a wish," and there are plenty of sayings about what you can do with a wish. Identify your dream, and then the work begins. The action begins. You can begin taking steps toward accomplishing the vision on your heart.

In the army, I learned to describe this as backward planning. You set a goal, then start moving backward until you get to the step you can do today. Sports Outreach did not just suddenly buy land and build buildings. I didn't just suddenly get on a plane to come to Uganda. Such moves took baby steps—lots of small pieces that build into something big. It's amazing what can happen when you follow God's calling and see what He can do through you.

One thing is certain: dreams don't happen without sacrifice. When you say "yes" to one thing, you also say "no" to something else. I need to be intentional and purposeful in my decisions and aware of what I say no to. Sacrifices will be made. I want my sacrifices to matter.

Brendan's hand on my back during prayer

Chapter 6

The Sacrifice Means It Matters

> He who would accomplish little must sacrifice little;
> he who would achieve much must sacrifice much; he
> who would attain highly must sacrifice greatly.

> - James Allen

As Stephanie and I prepared for our trip, we didn't realize how many things we had to give up. Because we said yes to Uganda, we had to say no to a lot of things. As our departure approached, the list grew.

One of our friends hosts a Super Bowl party every year. Her son is the same age as Andrew, and they are great friends. We have to drag them apart every time we get together. When we recognized our flight left at the same time the Super Bowl would kick off, our hearts dropped. Finding time with friends is a challenge, and it hurt to say goodbye to one of those infrequent opportunities. And for you sports fans, the game we missed was between New England and Seattle in Super Bowl XLIX (or Super Bowl 49 for the Roman numeral illiterate). The game ended with Seattle throwing an interception from the one-yard line to lose by four points. It was one of the most exciting games ever, and we were over the Atlantic for the whole thing.

I wasn't the only one sacrificing for this trip. Andrew tried to talk me out of going to Uganda so I could attend Donuts with Dads at his school. He gave up time, and free donuts, with his dad. That is a huge sacrifice for an eight-year-old.

One of the biggest events we missed was Brendan's twelfth birthday. Worse, it wasn't even the first time I missed his birthday. Brendan was born in 2003, when I was in the army. Later that year, I received orders to deploy to Iraq, and I left one month before his first birthday. The morning I flew out of El Paso remains one of the most painful moments of my life. My heart tore apart as I prepared to board the plane to Iraq. I chose to say goodbye in the parking lot, tears falling down my cheeks as I buckled my children into their car seats. I wouldn't do that simple task again for five months. My daughter, Lanie, only two and a half at the time, held out her cup of chocolate milk and offered it to me. "Chocolate milk, Daddy? Make you feel better." Her caring and sweet offer made the tears fall faster as I hugged her goodbye.

So here I was, eleven years later, missing another birthday. Because of the eight-hour time difference and the inconsistent internet access, I couldn't even call to wish him a happy birthday. I felt like the worst dad ever. To help me through that distress, I remembered our last night together. We attended church together, and the pastor asked our team to stand up so that he could pray over us. As the church reached their hands in our direction, I felt Brendan's hand on my back. Even though I would miss his birthday, he was praying for me. Just like Lanie and her chocolate milk, Brendan was doing what he could to show his love for me before I left.

The sacrifice means it matters.

Our trip to Uganda was important.

We were going to share the gospel with people who lived in the dark and had never heard about Jesus before. We would provide medical care and save lives.

God changed my heart and my perspective in Uganda. Before we left, I didn't know everything that would happen, but I knew the sacrifices we made were confirmation of the importance of our trip.

It's been said you can tell a lot about a person by going through their garbage. What a person will sacrifice tells you even more. You find out what they consider to be important and what they think is worthless. In our society, we tend to give from our surplus. We offer items we don't need or want. I don't take my favorite jacket to Goodwill, or my new pair of boots. I take clothes that don't fit, shoes I don't wear, or other stuff I don't use. It doesn't hurt to give that away.

Consider tithing. Many people don't give the first ten percent to hit the bank account. They wait to see what's left at the end of the month and give from that amount. If they can.

I gave up stuff I cared about to go to Uganda because I knew it was important. Even though it hurt, I did it because I knew we would impact lives. I said no to those things so that I could say yes to something else.

Don't we make these choices every day? Maybe you declined the promotion at work because it would take away too much time with your children. Or maybe you took the job offer, not realizing the impact it would have on the time with your family.

Our choices matter. We can spend the night watching TV because we're tired and just want to unplug. When we say yes to the TV, we say no to reading, talking with our family, or volunteering to help others. We can say we're too busy, but just about everything we have to do is a result of saying yes to something.

Every yes in one area of your life is a no in another area. You begin to see what is important to you by looking at what you sacrifice. What do you say "Yes" to? What does it keep you from? What will you say "No" to protect?

Going to Uganda required meaningful sacrifices, and not just from things that would happen while we were gone. I expected God to do significant things through me and to use me to advance His kingdom. I wanted to maximize this opportunity, and so I had to prepare before I left. As a Christian sharing the love of Jesus, spiritual forces would oppose me and try to keep me from completing my mission.

A soldier doesn't jump out of a plane naked and without a weapon. He wouldn't last long in a battle. A warrior prepares his uniform, checks his parachute, and trains with his weapon. A great deal of time and effort is put in to be physically ready. All the time spent in preparation is so he is ready to move the minute his boots hit the ground.

Abraham Lincoln said, "Give me six hours to chop down a tree and I will spend the first four sharpening my axe." I wanted to sharpen my axe through some of the spiritual disciplines, like fasting. Fasting is performed to show dependency on God by not eating for a period of time. Instead of eating, I prayed or read the Bible. I looked up Bible verses that talked about fasting. Isaiah 58 was a powerful passage for me:

> **Isaiah 58:6–8**: Is this not the fast that I choose: to loose the bonds of wickedness, to undo the straps of the yoke, to let the oppressed go free, and to break every yoke? Is it not for you to share your bread with the hungry and bring the homeless poor into your house; when you see the naked to cover him, and not to hide yourself from your own flesh? Then shall light break forth like the dawn, and your healing shall spring up speedily; your righteousness shall go before you; the glory of the Lord will be your rear guard.

The Israelites complained because they fasted but nothing happened. God responded by saying they were fasting in deed but not in their hearts. They didn't fast out of love, but as a show of how righteous they were. God wanted them to use their fast to feed the hungry, clothe the naked, and free the oppressed. If they fasted for those reasons, God promised the light would shine and healing would occur. As I prayed, I focused on the promises to see God's light shine in dark places and bring healing to a hurting people. He had already gone before us, and I wanted to see the glory of God as we ministered to the people of Uganda.

My final preparation occurred as the plane began the slow descent to the airport in Entebbe. I wanted to stand firm and step out with boldness. I put on my armor as I readied myself to go into battle.

> **Ephesians 6:10–18:** Finally be strong in the Lord and the strength of His might. Put on the whole armor of God, that you may be able to stand against the schemes of the devil. For we do not wrestle with flesh and blood, but against the rulers, against the authorities, against the cosmic powers over this present darkness, against the spiritual forces of evil in the heavenly places. Therefore, take up the whole armor of God, that you may be able to stand in the evil day, and having done all, to stand firm. Stand therefore, having fastened on the belt of truth, and having put on the breastplate of righteousness, and as shoes for your feet, having put on the readiness given by the gospel of peace. In all circumstances take up the shield of faith, with which you may extinguish all the flaming darts of the evil one;

and take the helmet of salvation and the sword of the spirit, which is the word of God, praying at all times in the Spirit, with all prayer and supplication.

The devil plans against us. We might think we fight with other people, even ourselves, but our true fight is against spiritual forces. I knew I would come under attack as I followed God's calling in Uganda. All my preparation was intended to ready myself to be able to stand firm when it happened. As our team transitioned from the poverty in Kampala to the devastation and tragedy in Gulu, the atmosphere within our team was transformed.

Evil had dominated this area for years and these people had witnessed and experienced unspeakable horrors. Wickedness was a way of life here; abuse and trauma were normal. Our struggle just got a lot more real.

Worship in the bus

Photo credit: Leigh Ann Loeblein

Chapter 7

Face to Face with the Impact of Evil

The story of your life is the story of the long
and brutal assault on your heart by the one who
knows what you could be and fears it.

- John Eldredge

Alone in our room in Gulu, Stephanie and I spent most of our time in heated exchange. Her frustration with the "constant religious stuff" reached an all-time high. The day had been hard for her since we hadn't sat together. "They're always singing those worship songs, or praying, or talking about Jesus. It feels like church camp."

My face flushed as I voiced my frustration. "Why do you always have to so critical?"

"I'm not being critical. I would like to listen to other music or talk about other things every once in a while."

My heart raced and my ears were blazing hot. "I hate this attitude you have. I'm sorry you don't feel a part of the team, but it's your own fault."

With hurt in her eyes and fire in her voice, she said, "Don't worry about me. You go do what you want. Sit where you want. Talk to whoever you want. I'll be just fine."

I had crossed a line. With a calmer tone, I backed away from my bristling statements. "I want to sit with you. I'm not going to leave you to sit by yourself. I just don't want to always isolate ourselves because you feel uncomfortable."

We reached a tentative truce and went to bed. Tossing and turning, we spent an uneasy night trying to sleep. At 3:00 a.m., I woke up covered in sweat, the air still and stale. The air conditioner was off. I tried to force it back into operation, but nothing worked. The windows wouldn't open, and I lay down in sweaty frustration.

I gave up at 4:45 a.m. as loud music blared from the courtyard below. Between the music and the stuffy heat of the room, sleep was hopeless. The tension from the fight with Stephanie added to the miserable sleeping conditions. I thought about trying to Skype Brendan, but the WiFi was on the same circuit as the air conditioners. Without electrical power, I was limited in what I could do. I prayed for a little while, for our trip, for our team, for those we would serve. I got out of bed and read a few chapters from the book of Acts. I wanted to see how the church started, how the gospel was shared. I felt unsure about what to say after someone accepts Jesus and asks for a new heart.

In my sleeplessness, I thought of the story of a young man from the book of I Samuel. Samuel is a boy learning from Eli how to be a priest. Samuel wakes in the middle of the night when he hears someone calling his name, so he gets up and asks Eli what he wants. Eli tells the lad, "I didn't call you. Go back to bed." A little while later, Samuel again hears his name being called, and reports to his mentor. "It wasn't me. Go back to bed." A third time, Samuel is lying there trying to sleep and hears someone call his name. "Samuel." When he goes to his teacher, Eli realizes it is God who called the boy. He told Samuel, "Go back. If you hear your name again, say 'Speak, Lord, for your servant listens.'"

When God called Samuel's name again, he did as Eli instructed, and the Lord began speaking to Samuel. Samuel would listen to God's voice throughout the rest of his life.

Many mornings when I wake up before my alarm goes off, I figure there must be a reason. God had a purpose in waking Samuel. Perhaps He also has a purpose in waking me; something for me to do, hear, or learn. I will pray and ask God to speak to me. I might read or write in my journal, listening for God's voice, to hear something I will need for that day.

On this morning, my efforts felt flat, and I didn't find what I was searching for. I had wanted start the day refreshed, but rest was beyond reach. Even after I gave up my search for sleep, I failed in my attempt to connect with God. My fists and jaw clenched in frustration as I waited for the sun to rise and our day to begin.

Stephanie got out of bed, our conversation icy in the heat of the room. I said a quick prayer as we prepared to go down for breakfast, "Father, let me get out of Your way. Do Your will through me, not just today, but every day." On our way to the dining room, we discovered the reason for the stifling atmosphere we experienced overnight. The power grid remains unstable in Gulu, and the hotel turns off electricity in the middle of the night. The whole team had an uneasy night, struggling with frustration and heat.

We walked into a tense and quiet dining room. In our previous mornings together, our team filled a room with the sounds of talking and laughing. Not this morning. The team was bleary-eyed and grumpy. I looked at Stephanie and wondered what to do. I wanted to sit and engage with the team, not sit in isolation. I also did not want Stephanie to feel abandoned. Meeting her eyes, I said, "I want to sit with you" under my breath. She gave me a quick nod, and followed me to an open spot at a table. The tension between us dissolved as we ate breakfast together. By the time we loaded the bus, we were back to normal. I held her hand as we headed off to Koro Farm.

The bus stopped at the gate to the farm and Bishop stood up to talk. Although Stephanie and I were reconnected, tension filled the bus. Faces were lined with stress and anxiety. Laughter was nonexistent. As Bishop looked at the tight faces surrounding him, he knew spiritual forces opposed our presence in Gulu, and we had to prepare for what we would face in the day ahead.

As Jesus did when tempted by the devil, we turned to the Bible to combat the oppressive atmosphere. We read several Bible verses to center our focus on what God called us to do. Missy read Ephesians 6:10–18, the same verses I had written on the way in. We would need the full armor of God to stand firm in the face of evil. We battled distraction, frustration, and weariness as we carried the gospel to these desperate, beaten-down people.

We were entering a different fight. In Kampala, much of the suffering was a result of extreme poverty. One man we had worked with always had a smile on his face. He seemed so positive, and we appreciated his uplifting spirit. Someone said it didn't look like he ever had a bad day. A darkness flickered over his face. Almost in a whisper, he said, "I have bad days." We asked him what a bad day looked like, wondering what could dampen his mood. He looked in our eyes. "The days I don't eat. Those are bad days." We gulped and averted our eyes as we glimpsed a bit of the struggle he faces. Bad days in Kampala are a constant fight for survival.

In Gulu, bad days look a lot different. Joseph Kony had terrorized these people for decades. His Lord's Resistance Army, the LRA, appeared out of nowhere from the bush to raid a village. During the attack, they took the children, some as young as eight years old, and ordered them to kill their parents. The boys became soldiers, and the girls were forced to become wives to the officers.

If they refused to kill their parents or to do whatever the LRA told them to do, they were killed. Over the next few days, we heard story after story of these heartbreaking events.

One young man told us he was kidnapped with his best friend. They were forced to be soldiers, although they never stopped trying to escape. One morning, he saw his friend, who had tried to escape, now held between two other soldiers. His commander called him to the front of the formation and handed him a tree limb as big as his arm. With a voice that must be obeyed, the officer instructed the boy to go over and beat his best friend to death with it. The young man knew if he resisted or even hesitated, both of them would be killed. He took the stick and followed his orders.

These child soldiers lived in constant fear during their time with the LRA. For years, they faced death, beatings, and rape. The few children who escaped found themselves outcast by their village because of the things they had done. Although the LRA departed northern Uganda several years ago, the young men and women they left behind continue to be imprisoned by the horror of their memories. Sexual abuse is rampant in this area. Their eyes are vacant, haunted by their past.

The plight of the Ugandan people is described with greater depth in *The Queen of Katwe* and *First Kill Your Family*. *The Queen of Katwe*, which I mentioned earlier, takes you into what life is like in the slums of Kampala. I recommend *First Kill Your Family*, by Peter Eichstaedt, for a first-hand account of the horrors inflicted upon northern Uganda. The LRA, refugee camps, and constant fear reshaped the people of this area, and Peter Eichstaedt tells their story with compassion and insight.

The fight in Gulu was not against poverty and dirty water. True evil plagued these people every day. Any woman over the age of twenty had likely been sexually abused. This society knew little of real love. The sole source of the love and healing they needed was Jesus. Jesus came to heal the broken hearted and set captives free (Isaiah 61:1, Luke 4:18). Satan tried to distract, frustrate, and diminish our impact on these people. The tension and frustration we experienced indicated his opposition to our calling.

In *Waking the Dead*, John Eldredge writes, "The story of your life is the story of the long and brutal assault on your heart by the one who knows what you could be and fears it." What assault have you faced? Maybe your father left you when you were a child. Now you have children and have no idea what to do. You have no experience to learn from, and may even be tempted to disappear. Oh, you won't leave, but work consumes you. Or sports. Or literally anything other than being a father. I mean, it's better to be a ghost than a failure, right?

Maybe you were abused by someone you trusted, and you vowed, "Never again." You keep everyone at a distance, staying safe. No one gets in. No one will ever have the chance. No one ever knows the real you. And all the time, your gift of encouraging and standing with others is suffocated.

More often than a frontal assault, like those situations, the enemy uses subtlety and sleight of hand. We find success in what we do and believe our success is proof of God's support. We lose sight of the importance of our calling as husband and father. We reach for more, bigger, higher, but lose what's right in front of us. Our accomplishments become the temptation drawing us away from what is most important.

We need to be aware of our tendency to create idols. You might not think of your idol as an idol, as you have never bowed down or prayed to a wooden statue. Our idols are much more sophisticated.

I discussed the topic of idols with Sal one day after a keeper of village idols came to faith in Jesus. We spoke about how odd the idea of idols seemed. "I am surprised to see people worshiping idols. It's not something we think about in the States. I talked with some of the guys about it. It's easy to look down on these people who worship statues made of wood and stone. We treat them like they are uncivilized. The thing is, we have idols too. We just call them things like fun, money, career, or security."

Sal responded, "You're exactly right. We create idols when we depend on those things more than we depend on God. Even if it's a good thing, what we cling to the most can become our idols."

Sal's words brought understanding and insight like a bolt of lightning to my brain. I saw so many idols I created. Success at work. Validation from others. Even volunteering at church. I used those things to indicate whether I was a success or a failure. And like all the other idols, I needed to knock them down and demolish them.

Sometimes we want a good thing too much, and it becomes a god in our lives. It could be our jobs. It could be our families. It could even be working in the church. When the desire or activity takes a priority over our relationship with our true Father, we craft an idol. Once it is recognized, it must be removed.

When you become aware of the idol or assault, don't face it by yourself. As we did in Uganda, turn to the Bible to find the truth in your circumstances. Focus on Jesus, not on the problems. Be purposeful in your actions. Ground yourself in the foundation of prayer.

After we were done reading and praying, the bus felt brighter. The air was cleaner and the pressure lifted. We continued to our destination and sang a song of victory.

Ever Glorious
Elevation Worship

You are gracious in majesty,
You're the mighty and humble King
You have always been,
You will always be
You were crowned with my sin and shame,
You're enthroned in the highest praise
You have always been,
You will always be

(chorus) So we lift the cross, His banner over us
For the Lord our God is ever glorious.

And the heavens shout, declaring over us,
That the Lord our God is ever glorious.

You are constant forevermore.
You're exalted and still adored
You have always been,
You will always be.
You surrendered in victory.
You are risen to life in me.
You have always been,
You will always be.

(chorus) So we lift the cross, His banner over us
For the Lord our God is ever glorious.

And the heavens shout, declaring over us,
That the Lord our God is ever glorious.

(Bridge) Ever glorious,
is the name of Christ
And His love endures,
ever glorious.

(chorus) So we lift the cross, His banner over us
For the Lord our God is ever glorious.

And the heavens shout, declaring over us,
That the Lord our God is ever glorious.

Although we arrived in the middle of the song, we kept singing, hands lifted, eyes closed as we raised His banner and protection over us. We brought more than medicine to these people. We offered ourselves, and brought the love of Jesus to a dying world. We came face to face with an evil presence during those days, but the power of Christ in us would bring victory in the darkness.

Koro Farm Worship Center

Photo credit: Leigh Ann Loeblein

Chapter 8

The Hands and Feet of Jesus

I get tired of taking my Isaacs up the mountain.

- Jonathan Ryan

Patients gathered under white canopies and waited for the medical clinic to begin. As the sun rose higher in the sky, shade became precious, and people would crowd together in the shadows around the worship center. I walked with Bishop around the perimeter of Koro Farm and told him about my argument the night before with Stephanie, and how frustrated I felt.

I also described my struggle to find a sweet spot during this trip. I looked around and it seemed everyone had found a place or job they loved. I hadn't. I felt like I wasted my nursing skills by not doing nursing stuff. I hadn't found a place to call home. Every day started the same. While the rest of the team organized their areas, I wandered around looking for something to do. I worried I was missing something.

He laughed and said, "I guarantee you no one else thinks that. From what I see, you aren't struggling in any way. You see the need and respond. My friend, you have been the hands and feet of Jesus on this trip."

As he spoke these words of encouragement, an image penetrated my mind. I imagined applying a blood-pressure cuff to a patient in Katwe. As I patted the patient on the shoulder to reassure him, I saw my hands had nail holes in them. Shaken by the power of this vision, tears filled my eyes. I told Bishop of the affirmation and reassurance I received.

We overuse the phrase "hands and feet of Jesus" within Christian circles. At least, we use it without really thinking about what it means. I want people to see Jesus through me. I want them to see His love reflected in my eyes. When I pat a child on the head, or help her up from the ground, I want to touch with the hands of Jesus. Many people have never experienced true love in their lives, and I want to make the most of my opportunities to show them the love of Jesus. The image I received changed the way I approached, not just this trip, but my life. When people see me, I want them to see Jesus.

This attitude is easy to have on a short-term mission trip. I was away from my job, my kids, all the stress and responsibilities I face every day. I could focus all my attention and energy into this effort. It becomes more difficult in the rush of my hectic life. It's frustrating.

You don't have to go to overseas, or on a mission trip, to be the hands and feet of Jesus. Shouldn't we do that every day? When our kids are getting on our last nerve, we should want them to see Jesus in our response. If we feel betrayed and alone, we know Jesus felt the same way and can look to him for answers. Do the people around you see Jesus when they watch you drive? Play sports? Speak to your wife?

I wish I could say I did this well. I don't. As Paul describes:

Romans 7:18b-20, 24a (HCSB): For the desire to do what is good is with me, but there is no

ability to do it. For I do not do the good that I
want to do, but I practice the evil that I do not
want to do. Now if I do what I do not want, I am
no longer the one doing it, but it is the sin that
lives in me...What a wretched man I am!

If this is how Paul felt, how much more will we experience
the same level of frustration? We know what we want to do, but
we struggle to do it. And when we blow it, again and again, the
feeling of failure overwhelms and devastates us. As husbands. As
fathers. As men. As Paul said, "What a wretched man I am!"

But we can't stop there. If we do, we find ourselves locked in a
cycle of failure and condemnation. In the next breath, Paul shows
us the way out of the cycle:

> **Romans 7:25-8:2:** Thanks be to God, who
> delivers me through Jesus Christ our Lord! . . .
> Therefore, there is now no condemnation for
> those who are in Christ Jesus, because through
> Christ Jesus the law of the Spirit who gives life has
> set you free from the law of sin and death.

Jesus had said the same thing in John 3:17: "For God did not
send His Son into the world to condemn the world, but in order
that the world might be saved through Him." Salvation without
condemnation. What a concept!

I am always so quick to criticize myself every time I make a
mistake. "I blew it. Again. I'm a failure. Why do I always mess
things up?" I know I can't be the only one. Ever blow up on the
golf course after a bad shot? Want to hide your head in shame after
a poor review? Whenever you disappoint yourself or fail to live
up to your standards, do you label yourself a failure? If so, let me
encourage you to change the way you think in those situations.

We live in a manufactured reality of shame and disappointment, even though the gospel message tells us differently. The good news is there is no condemnation!

Do we *want* to keep messing up? Of course not. Is this some sort of kitchen pass to do whatever we want? Still no. It's the simple offer of grace. We can confess our sin, repent of our errors, and try again with a heart full of the freedom of forgiveness, unburdened by condemnation from past failures.

As I continue on my journey of being the hands and feet of Jesus, every day is a new day. A prayer found on St. Patrick's breastplate includes the same sentiment:

Christ with me, Christ before me, Christ behind me,
Christ in me, Christ beneath me, Christ above me,
Christ on my right, Christ on my left,
Christ when I lie down, Christ when I sit down,
Christ in the heart of everyone who thinks of me,
Christ in the mouth of everyone who speaks of me,
Christ in the eye that sees me,
Christ in the ear that hears me.

I arise today
Through the mighty strength
Of the Lord of creation.

What would happen if we prayed this every morning? Or, even better, every time we wanted to react in a sinful way? If only we could pause in the moment and pray this reminder of who we are. Just like soldiers put on their equipment before going out to battle, we should protect ourselves with prayer before we start our day.

Bishop and I walked to the prayer tent, where I met Esther, Aloysius' wife. I told her about the frustration and fear I had experienced. With a gentle smile, she responded in her soft Ugandan accent, "You cannot live in fear. You have to trust God to do what you cannot. You can't change anyone's heart, only God can. You need to trust Him to work. Clear your heart of any doubt or fear."

She described the girls who came to Christine's House. All of them had suffered sexual abuse, and many were pregnant as a result. They were outcasts in their villages, unwanted and unloved, but Esther welcomed them all to Christine's House. One day Esther was cooking when one of the girls spilled boiling water down her back. Eyes wide in pain and anger, Esther wanted to yell at her and send her home. But when she looked at the girl who cowered before her, tears filled her eyes and she couldn't. She knew the life the girl would go back to. Esther told me, "The ones we love the most create the hardest tests. We care about what happens to them. We are invested in their lives. We are the most tested, the most frustrated, when things don't follow the smooth, ideal path that we had envisioned."

My mind drifted back to the idea of sacrifice. Esther sacrificed a great deal for these girls that she loved so much. Because of her investment into their lives, what happened to them mattered to her. But sometimes the girls didn't respond like she hoped. They abandoned their children. They returned to the village to start the cycle of abuse again. When this happened, Esther would pick up the devastated pieces of her heart and turn to her loving Father to heal them so she could continue her work.

How do we respond when things don't go as planned? How do we react when what we are asked to sacrifice is the one thing we want more than anything? I remembered the story of Abraham and Isaac. For almost seventy-five years, Abraham longed to have a son, someone to continue the family. God had promised him his descendants would outnumber the stars in the sky. After

God's promise, Abraham waited twenty-five years before holding Isaac in his arms. What joy he must have had after showing such perseverance all those years.

And what a shock it had to be when God told Abraham to sacrifice Isaac. Can you imagine? The one thing Abraham wanted more than anything else, and God wanted him to kill it.

What would my response have been? Probably not as submissive as Abraham's.

"But God, you promised!" Disbelief.

"After all the time I waited, and now this?" Anger.

"No. Please, God, anything but that." Bargaining.

Isn't this how we respond when life doesn't go as we planned? I came to Uganda with this idea of how things would go. When they didn't go as I thought they should, I became frustrated. I felt lost.

God calls us to do things we are not comfortable doing. Just look at Abraham, Moses, Peter, even Jesus. They all said variations of, "Anything but that," quickly followed by, "Not my will, but yours." Why would our experience be any different?

Jonathan Ryan once said, "I get tired of taking my Isaacs up the mountain." Every time we sacrifice a dream in submission, another Isaac shows up. The things we want most have to be sacrificed. Well, almost. At the end of the story, Isaac didn't end up dying on the altar. It's not the son that has to be sacrificed; it's our sense of control.

God was checking Abraham's heart and asking him, "Do you trust me? Will you submit to my plan? Is your faith in me, or in what you see?" He asks us the same questions. We walk in situations where we are uncomfortable in order to show our dependence on Him. As David writes in Psalm 23, "Even though I walk through the valley of the shadow of death, I will fear no evil, for you are with me." When everything around you looks dark, what do you hold on to? Are you able to live like David and Abraham and follow God through those places?

As I prayed with Esther, a sense of peace surrounded my heart. I walked out of the tent without the pressure to perform or complete tasks to succeed. I was free to follow the guidance of the Spirit and help where I was needed. Before I knew it, morning was over and lunch arrived from the hotel.

We set up chairs in a circle in the middle of the medical clinic and sat down as a team. As I ate, I felt hundreds of eyes on me. I looked around at the people waiting. How many of them had nothing to eat? I looked at the tray full of food in my hands. This might be more food than they ate all day. I had so much, and it felt gluttonous to eat it all. I ate what I needed and asked Sam, our guide, if anyone needed my leftovers. He laughed and said, "There's no such thing as leftovers in Uganda." He took what remained and gave it out.

The rest of the day went by in a blur as I spent most of the afternoon helping Stephanie in the pharmacy. I wanted to put our fight behind us, and our time together helped reestablish our joy in being here. The afternoon flew by, and we headed back to the hotel. The bus was alive with chatter as we looked forward to Sunday morning and going to an African church.

Saturday was a turning point in my trip, and I saw God do amazing things over the next few days. I focused less on what others thought and expected of me, and focused more on the job right in front of me. I moved away from performing nursing tasks and became involved in providing spiritual support and encouragement to my team and the Ugandans. I began the process of stripping away my expectations in order to open my heart to follow God's direction. I wrote in my journal that night: "Every person I touch, I touch with Jesus' hands. I need to look at them with love, think of them with love, speak to them in love. I need to worry less about what others will think and only what my Creator thinks. I don't want to land in Charlotte with any regrets, so I need to step into my calling."

We started Sunday where we finished our Saturday, at the ministry center at Koro Farm. What had been a medical clinic was now set up as a church. When we arrived, Bishop asked if anyone would be willing to share a brief testimony. When no one offered, I raised my hand. I don't shy away from speaking, especially when it's talking about what God has done in my life. My real problem is knowing when to shut up. Jimmy, George, and Brittany volunteered to share their stories as well. While this opportunity was spontaneous, it was amazing to see a theme develop in what we said.

We entered the building to find the service already in progress. Every eye was on us as we found our seats. As the only white people there, we attracted a lot of attention. After a couple of songs, the leader asked us to come up to share. With butterflies in my stomach, I walked to the podium, praying that God would speak His words through me.

I shared about the mistakes I had made in my life, mistakes that led to my divorce. I felt unworthy and unwanted, too dirty and messed up to be welcome in church. But I was wrong. My God is an everlasting Father who runs to me with open arms. He welcomed me, no matter what was in my past. It's a picture from the story Jesus told about the prodigal son. A rich man had two sons, and one day his youngest son told his father he wanted to cash out his inheritance and go out on his own. The father gave half of his possessions to him and the young man set out into the world. In no time at all, this son spent all he had on parties and wild living. He found himself starving, taking care of some pigs, jealous of how well they ate. The son decided to return to his father and beg him to work as a servant in his house. As he approached the house, his father saw him and ran to him. He was overjoyed to see his son return to him, and embraced him, welcoming him home as a son. I felt the same way when I returned to church years ago, and God told me, "I'm so glad you're home." The story of the prodigal son is my story, and has had a powerful impact on my life.

As the others got up to speak, the theme of father continued to come to the surface. One had a great role model. Another felt ashamed of his performance as a father. One testimony was especially powerful in this culture, as the person described an abusive relationship. This story resonated with people who had known only trauma and abuse through their lives.

Unrehearsed, our stories set the stage for what Bishop would say. He preached what the Bible declares about God's children, using words like redeemed, holy, and blameless. The Bible resonates with messages of God's love for His children, culminating in the arrival of Jesus. The Bible is a long letter from a loving Father who desires our love in return. To a people who had experienced a great deal of abuse and loss, we spoke about our gracious and merciful Father.

Although the service was three hours long, in a building with plastic chairs and no air conditioning, no one was ready for it to stop. We were reenergized for our last two medical clinics. Filled with new life from our worship, we changed our clothes, ready to be the hands and feet of Jesus and take light into a dark world.

The crowd gathered in Lajwatek

Chapter 9

Do You Believe in Miracles?

When Jesus landed and saw the large crowd, He had
compassion on them and He healed their sick.

- Matthew 14:14 (NIV)

We arrived at the village of Lajwatek in the early afternoon.
People filled the tent and packed into every available shady spot.
Silence filled the bus as we entered the village and observed the
size of the crowd awaiting us. Like the slow thaw of a frozen
lake, realization crept through my brain. Despite seeing large
numbers of people in our clinics, our efforts in Uganda barely
made a dent in the overwhelming need. Even now, more than two
hundred people waited to be seen and we had precious few hours
of sunlight left. Facing an insurmountable task, we shuffled off
the bus and began to set up.

As the team prepared the pharmacy and provider areas, I
circled the small area to pray. A ramshackle playground was
outside the two one-room school buildings. The heat of the
early afternoon sun beat down as I walked through the dust. I
stared at the crowd as I prayed for our team and our mission.
I had no idea how we would be able to care for all of them by
nightfall.

I remembered a story Jimmy shared about his mission trip to Nicaragua. Toward the end of the trip, his team cooked a dinner for the church. They bought enough food and supplies for one hundred people: plates, cups, silverware. They had one hundred of everything. Happy voices filled the room as they cooked and set up this special dinner. When they opened the doors to begin letting people in, the line stretched around the tiny church. With smiles and grateful hearts, they welcomed the hungry crowd to their feast. The stack of plates grew shorter as the line continued to move. Jimmy glanced at the rest of his team as the last plate was taken.

The next person in line waited as Jimmy went around the dining area looking for empty plates. He gathered them up and washed them for the people still waiting in line. He poked his head out of the door to see how many folks remained. His heart fell as he saw the line continue around the building. He raced back into the kitchen to find they still had food to serve.

He and his team dashed around the dining room and cleared the tables of used utensils. A quick wash and rinse, and they stacked the supplies back at the beginning of the line. Jimmy began to get nervous, worried about what would happen if they ran out of food. They didn't want to disappoint anyone who came in.

Once more, the stack of plates disappeared, and still the line stretched out. Again they retrieved and washed the plates, setting them out to feed the remaining people in line. Jimmy's team broke down in tears as they kept serving. Even though people kept coming, they still had food. Everyone ate. Food was left over. It didn't make sense. They fed more than three hundred people with food bought for one hundred. As Jimmy shared the story with me, his eyes filled with tears at the wonder of the miracle.

I looked at the crowd of people waiting for us in Lajwatek. I didn't know how we could take care of all of them. We needed a miracle. We needed the strength to push through the day as we became overwhelmed with the stories we heard. Many of us struggled with the emotional pressure of knowing our trip was coming to a close. The next day was our final medical clinic. None of us wanted it to end. As the heat and emotions ran high, I read what the Bible said about miraculous provision: "When Jesus landed and saw the large crowd, He had compassion on them and He healed their sick (Matthew 14:14, NIV)."

Whoa. I took a step back as I read those words. We faced the same situation Jesus did. When we arrived in the bus, it would have been easy to see the large crowd and give in to discouragement and fatigue. But how did Jesus respond to the large crowd? With compassion and healing. We needed to follow his example. I went around to my team and shared this encouragement to keep going.

I wish I responded with compassion more often. Maybe I'm not facing a large crowd every day, but I feel overwhelmed. I know what my to-do list looks like before I get to work. When I try to rest at home, my kids demand my attention. The needs and demands on my life feel like more than I can handle.

One definition of burnout is when the demands are higher than the resources available. Burnout is not confined to work. Every role we play is susceptible to this problem. Family needs, activities and functions we attend leave us tired, angry, and burned out. Every time we turn around, we get pulled in another direction. When we can't take it anymore, we check out or explode.

I could write another book based on the effectiveness with which Jesus responded to the demands placed on Him. For now I'll focus on the compassion. The Greek word is much more powerful than we imagine in English. It describes an urge, a movement in one's bowels. Without being too graphic, imagine that feeling of gastric distress. The need to evacuate. To take action to avoid disaster. That is the depth of Christ's compassion. A powerful urge in His inmost being demands action.

How can we respond with compassion? One way is to see the person behind the request. Jesus saw the large crowds. He saw their needs. When my kids pull on me, trying to get my attention, I don't see them. I see the stack of work I need to do. I see the things around the house I need to fix. I feel overwhelmed and snap at them for always asking me to play basketball or video games when I have so much to do. Not much compassion in my usual response. For them or for me.

And it's not just the kids. It can be my wife. My pastor. My boss or colleagues at work. Even my friends. Always asking me for one more thing than I feel I can do.

The Bible doesn't suggest that Jesus looked at a to-do list. He realized the person isn't the interruption. The person is the mission.

Another way we can respond with compassion is to pursue purpose. Jesus did those things that only He could do. If we spent more time filtering out the less important tasks, we would have capacity to fulfill our unique purposes. Father. Husband. Son. Friend. Show compassion to yourself by saying no sometimes, especially if you can say yes to something more critical.

The last element I noticed is how Jesus engaged. He touched people. He looked them in the eye. He met their needs. Right before Jesus fed all these people, he had learned of the death of his cousin, John the Baptist. He tried to get away from the crowds, but they followed Him. I bet He was tired and grieving, and I suspect the last thing He wanted to see was a horde of needy people.

But He had compassion. He healed them and then He fed them. He saw the need was so great He was moved in the depths of His being to do something about it.

If I did that, I would realize fifteen minutes playing basketball with my son would matter more than anything I could accomplish around the house in the same time. Maybe I don't need to go to a meeting every night of the week so that I can spend one night with my wife. I can look at an interruption as an opportunity, not a frustration.

To connect with the meaning and purpose in our lives, we have to engage with the people around us in a compassionate way. When the demands seem overwhelming, we turn to our limitless God to show us the way through. We need His wisdom to discern what is important. We need His strength to move when we want to check out. When we submit our desires to His will, miracles happen.

Just like Jimmy and the dinner in Nicaragua, just like Jesus feeding the five thousand, we were able to see every patient in the village. In less than six hours, we saw 278 patients and nine salvations. It was a wonderful day of communion with the Spirit, and the fog that had plagued me the previous day was nowhere to be seen.

I can't leave Lajwatek without telling you about Esther (not Aloysius' wife from Koro Farm). A few years ago, Esther became ill. She kept getting sicker, and no one in her village knew what to do. The village leader decided to send for Aloysius to come pray over her. A messenger left the village by foot and walked to where Aloysius was. This process took several days, and by the time Aloysius returned to the village, Esther had died. No pulse, no breathing. Nothing. Her funeral was planned for the next day.

Aloysius did not know this. He knew someone was sick, and he had been called to pray for her. He looked around the village, but saw no one. The villagers hid in their huts, afraid to tell him he had wasted his time. Aloysius entered Esther's hut and found her lying on the floor. He thought, "Wow, she looks really bad." He knelt down beside her, held her hand and prayed. Nothing happened. He felt like he had to call deeper, so he kept praying. He called her name. "Esther, wake up!" Sweat broke out on his forehead as he persisted in asking God for healing and deliverance. Suddenly, Esther gave a little cough and woke up. Aloysius helped her to stand, and they walked outside. When the villagers saw them emerge from the hut, they came out of hiding. What was intended to be a funeral became a feast of celebration.

This walking miracle came to our clinic, and, as she shared her story, a small group of people gathered to listen. When she finished, we stared at her in silence. Esther and Aloysius continued talking as we came to grips with what we had just heard. It sounded unbelievable. But after all I had seen, heard and experienced, I believed it.

Have you ever stopped to think about just how strange the Christian faith appears to be? I thought about how I circled the village, praying. I was struck by how strange this must look. This white guy, walking around this small village, speaking words and expecting things to happen as a result. Even something as simple as prayer is a strange thing to a non-believer.

A friend of mine works with a couple guys who claim to be atheists. He couldn't understand why they made such a big deal when he prayed over his food at lunch. We grew up in church and don't see prayer as abnormal. But for someone who doesn't believe in God, seeing someone pray over their meal appears as farfetched as believing Harry Potter to be a true story.

Christians pray to God and expect things to happen as a result. We believe the Bible, which has story after story of strange things happening. God spoke the world into existence. The whole earth was flooded. God talks to people. People survived a fiery furnace and a lions' den. A virgin became pregnant and gave birth to the Son of God. Jesus healed lepers, the blind, and the sick. He even raised people from the dead. He fed thousands from one person's lunch. When Jesus died, somehow all of our sinful behavior was placed on His shoulders. After He died, He came back to life, and now lives in heaven somewhere. We believe communion and baptism actually do something. That's a lot of weird stuff.

Does prayer appear any different than waving a wand and casting a spell? We say some words, and expect things to happen. Sure, it might not be turning a toadstool into a teacup, but healing cancer is a pretty impressive event. Deliverance, restoration, healing, and forgiveness are more difficult and more powerful than anything any wizard in any story ever did. If we want to be the light to a dark world, we need to understand how we appear and embrace the strange. The biggest miracle of all, the defeat of death, occurs through these unique beliefs.

After the clinic, with the light beginning to fade, Stephanie and I went for a short walk through the village, hand in hand as the sun set. One of the villagers allowed us to go into her mud hut, which was a very special privilege. These circular lodgings with thatched roofs were everywhere in northern Uganda, and we were excited to take a look inside. We saw her bathroom, which was two bricks next to a hole in the ground. They would stand on the bricks, squat, and, well, you get the picture. Cardboard was next to the hole, and that was what they wiped with. Ouch! They even had an outdoor shower. The showering person would stand on a floor of bricks, and someone would pour the water over them.

We entered the kitchen hut, where they cooked their food over an open fire. The smoke went out through the thatched roof, and the walls were black with soot. The men and women had separate huts, clothes hanging from clotheslines strung from one side to the other. The only light present came from the doors, or leaked through where the walls met the roof. It was really dark inside. For us anyway. I'm sure the Ugandans could see perfectly well. It was a tremendous honor for this woman to let us into her home, and we gave her a scarf as a gift of thanks.

At dinner that night, I felt the sadness growing in anticipation of our final day of medical clinics. While we had done so much for so many, the need remained great. I prayed for an extra portion of the Spirit to focus and see the work we had done, and not what still remained. I prayed for a happy goodbye, not a sad one. Tomorrow would prove to be one of the most incredible events I've been part of, so I believe that my prayers were answered.

The village of Pugwini hosted the last clinic of our trip. Eyes were downcast and red rimmed with the emotion of the day. We wound our way through the dirt roads to the village of Pugwini the next morning. Driving to a village in the bush is a lot different than driving in the US. The roads are all dirt; there are no street signs or buildings to help navigate the winding roads. All we saw were trees, shoulder-high grass, and some rocks. Yet our bus driver never seemed to waver or get confused. He knew exactly what road to take and how to get us to where we were going. We joked around and asked if he would get lost if someone cut down a tree or cut the grass. With a serious look on his face, he said, "Yes. That is exactly what would happen. It is not pleasant." Our Western comforts and culture take so many things for granted. We struggle to imagine how to live in these conditions. I was thankful we didn't get lost in the bush. We wouldn't stand a chance out there.

Like Lajwatek, we arrived to find a crowd waiting for us. When we saw the people, I felt a sense of dread fall over the group. How could we see all these people? How hot would it get today? This is our sixth clinic in seven days—how can we have the energy to get through it? After a deep breath and a prayer, we unloaded the bus and got started. While we had done so much for so many, the need remained great. I circled the village and prayed for strength to get through our final day together. I asked God to give us a happy goodbye.

The clinic opened, and patients processed through. I went to the prayer tent to pray for the people we would see. We asked God to help our team to accomplish the goals and mission for today. We prayed for people we would never see. I poured out my heart to God, to ask His blessings on the day, our team and every person my eyes could see.

Soon, one of the providers brought a patient to us who wanted to accept Jesus. Using the cube, we shared the gospel message with him, and he came to know Jesus. We prayed with him and welcomed him into our family. As soon as we finished praying with him, another patient came to talk to us, and the same thing happened. Over and over, we shared, prayed, and celebrated another changed heart. The Spirit moved powerfully through the village.

The morning flew by, and suddenly it was time for lunch. We wolfed down our food and got back to work. Later in the afternoon, Steve brought out a young man and said he wanted to accept Jesus. The heat of the afternoon sun placed a premium on shelter, and we had no room under the prayer tent as people crowded into whatever shade they could find. The soccer field in the center of the village looked to be a quiet place, so we sat down on the pitch to talk.

This kid looked about twelve years old. As I showed him the cube and talked about Jesus, more children wandered up and sat down. I got to the end and asked if they wanted to take Jesus as their Savior. The boy I started talking to said yes, so Steve took him aside to pray. The other children said they wanted to hear the whole story.

Reuben sat next to me as I started over. As I spoke, I tried to look each one of the children in the eyes. I knew the world they had been born into and the stories of the people around them. I also knew there was One who could overcome all the evil they would experience. I came to the end of the story, and asked those who wanted to trust in Jesus to raise their hands.

I gasped as most of them raised their hands. Reuben choked out "Praise God" as tears rolled down his face. Through my own choked up emotions, I led them in a prayer to ask Jesus to give them a new heart. I looked at these precious little children as I prayed and was amazed at the focus and intensity they displayed. Hands in tight little fists held over their eyes. Eyes closed in peaceful innocence and their hands held in perfect praying position. Hearts and lives changed in a moment as they put their trust in Jesus.

When we finished praying, I lifted my hands in the air and smiled as I exclaimed, "Welcome to the family!" I told them we were now brothers and sisters, and I was so happy to be in their family. Children are very important to Jesus, and I read to them how Jesus told his disciples to let the children come to Him. I handed these young ones over to the interpreter, who could connect them with a church in the community. They would need people surrounding them to help them grow in their faith.

I stumbled away, stunned and amazed by what had happened. I was blown away to be used by God to bring His light to these little ones, and I prayed they would grow up with God's protection and would be a changed generation for their villages.

God allowed me to participate in His miracles. The greatest miracle occurs when a heart of stone becomes a heart of flesh. When a dead heart comes to life. The angels rejoice when one lost soul is rescued. Heaven hosted a massive party while we were in Pugwini.

It's easy for Western missionaries to provide a parachute Christianity. I could drop in, do some stuff and disappear back to my normal life. The time might be tough and strenuous, but I don't have to change afterward. My life can go back to normal. But we didn't want to drop in, preach, and then disappear without any follow up.

The Ugandans we worked with live that life every day. When I left, I returned to my car, running water, grocery stores, and paved roads. They remained in the struggle. One hundred and sixty people accepted Jesus during our trip. We can't abandon them. It's up to the people in Uganda to help these new Christians walk in their new faith, help them in their struggles, and battle with them when life gets messy.

Our day started to wrap up, but we had one more moment awaiting us. Many of our Ugandan brothers and sisters would return to Kampala, and we would not see them before we left for Paraa the next morning. We wanted to honor and thank them for all they had done, so Bishop arranged for a foot-washing ceremony to take place by the village well. After the clinic closed, everyone gathered under the tents used to cover the people for much of the day. Several chairs were under the tents, and basins full of clean water. Bishop spoke for a few minutes and shared the results of the day and the trip. We ended our trip with our biggest clinic, seeing 472 patients, and forty-six people accepted Jesus as Savior! For our entire mission, we recorded more than two thousand patients, and 162 new believers, in only five and a half days of clinics. We celebrated what God did in this community through us. We knew it was now up to God to use our Ugandan counterparts to continue the work.

The foot-washing ceremony recognized the work and sacrifice our brothers and sisters make in Uganda. We wanted to honor them, not just in what they did with us that week, but in the life that they live. Bishop invited any of the Ugandans to come to a seat if they wanted to participate, and anyone who wanted to wash their feet was welcome. Participation was voluntary. I'm pretty sure everyone jumped in wholeheartedly. We washed and prayed for our helpers, volunteers, interpreters, providers. Without them, our mission would have failed. Without them, we would not have accomplished all that we did.

As I washed their feet, I spoke over them, telling them how beautiful are the feet that bear good news and explaining how they brought the good news of Jesus with them. Samuel, whom I worked with in the pharmacy and is now in medical school to become a neurosurgeon. Sophie, who worked so closely with Stephanie in the pharmacy. The woman who worked in our registration area, whose feet were deformed from birth and walked with crutches. Tears filled my eyes as I spoke life and blessing over these servants. My voice caught in my throat when Stephanie washed the feet as I prayed over them.

Aloysius was one of the last people to participate. As Bishop washed his feet, many of us gathered around to pray over him. I thanked God for this man and the heart he had for the people of Uganda. I prayed for God's continued presence as he became a powerful tool for the gospel, not just in Gulu, or only in Uganda, but for all of Africa. I opened my eyes and saw his wife Esther receiving a similar treatment nearby. Stephanie joined the group surrounding Esther, laying a hand on Esther's shoulder as others prayed over her. At that point, I lost control of my emotions and walked away weeping with thankfulness for everything I had experienced and observed during my time there.

Physically and emotionally exhausted, before I crawled into bed that night, I wrote in my journal: "God used me to share the gospel and sow seeds in so many lives this week. After a difficult beginning, the past two days have felt very Spirit-led. Thank you, Father, for using me. Thank you for the privilege of fighting for your kingdom. Thank you for my new friends, brothers and sisters. Please honor the commitments made today. Lock up their hearts and help them to follow you all the days of their lives."

I don't know how you can go on a trip like this and return unchanged. We go on these trips thinking we are going to make a difference and change the world for someone, but I found out I was among those forever changed.

Elephant selfies

Photo credit: Leigh Ann Loeblein

Chapter 10

Taking Uganda Home

Experience isn't the best teacher. Evaluated
experience is the best teacher.

- John Maxwell

The next morning dawned bright and hot, as most mornings seem to in February in Uganda. The team was quiet, spent from the days of furious physical activity and exhausted from pouring out our hearts. An air of sadness loomed as our primary mission was over, and we began preparing for reentry to Western civilization.

At the same time, we looked forward to some down time. What we had seen and experienced over the past week was intense, and we needed time and a safe space to process what happened. We wanted to ponder the things God had done in us and through us. We packed the bus after breakfast and loaded up for our trip to the Paraa Safari Lodge where we would spend the next two nights. As the bus rolled along, the noise level increased as the excitement built in anticipation of the next two days.

You might be wondering what place a safari has with a mission trip. You might think we wasted time and days we could have done more, seen more people, and delivered more care. More than a couple people on our team wished we held a medical clinic instead. It is a difficult decision.

Looking back, I see how critical this pause was. Reintegration into Western culture would be a shock. Like a scuba diver returning to the surface, we had to take it slowly. We needed time together as we dealt with what we had seen and experienced. This down time was a necessity for our own growth and sanity.

No one slept on the road to Paraa. The closer we traveled to our destination, the more animals we saw. Water buffalo, giraffes, birds, and monkeys. The biggest excitement came from seeing an elephant standing under a tree. The elephant looked so much darker, greyer, and more real than any elephant I had seen before. It was beautiful and awesome to see the animals in their natural environment.

I also saw different varieties of what was basically a deer scattered throughout the area. I was told they were antelope, bushbuck, waterbuck, gazelle, dik-dik, impalas, oribi, and kob, just to name a few of the species. I couldn't tell them apart, so I just called them "deer-like." While I may not be able to name them, I noticed how calm they were as our bus roared past. They stood just a couple feet off the road. Alert, but not scared. Vigilant, but not paranoid.

Lunch was ready soon after we arrived, and we ate on a balcony overlooking the Nile far below. Our rooms were ready after lunch, and our team went in different directions for a short time. My desire was to rest in our room or swim in the pool, but Stephanie wanted to explore the lodge. Although she was one of the people who wished for another clinic day, she was excited to be at Paraa and couldn't wait to see the animals and wander around. I put my own desires aside to spend time with my bride.

As we explored, my anger flared when she talked to me about returning to work. She told me, "You usually have a hard time getting back into the flow of work after you take a break. I want you to think about it so you can be ready when we get home."

I retorted, "You wanted to take a walk to lecture me?" My hurt feelings triggered a response of frustration and anger, designed to escalate our discussion and lead to a fight. "I could be resting right now, but I am out here sweating because you wanted to talk to me about work? I don't need you to manage me."

Despite my antagonistic response, Stephanie displayed patience and calm. She didn't take the bait. Her kind response to my barbed answer turned our conversation in a positive direction, and allowed us to enjoy our time together.

I wish I acted more like those deer-like animals standing next to the road. I feel scared of life changing and things not working out like I planned. I act like a bull, raging and running things down. Other times, I choose to respond like a possum, curling up in a ball and pretending I'm dead. I am tired of reacting and running away with every sound I hear, every "car" that comes bouncing down the road.

I want to be more like the deer. Watch what approaches and take every thought captive as 2 Corinthians 10:5 instructs. Test thoughts and situations to see what is going on and where it comes from. If it's from God, I allow it through and into my life. If it's not from God, I can prepare and respond appropriately. I want to live a life of preparation, not of panic. Awareness, not anxiety.

As we walked around Paraa, it felt like we stepped into a movie scene. Baboons ran around the property and through the hotel. The pool overlooked the Nile River, where elephants and hippos cooled off in the heat of the day. The setting was a surreal contrast to the poverty and trauma we had so recently experienced.

In preparation for our final team debriefing, Bishop asked us a couple questions. "First, consider why God brought you here. Second, what does God want you to do with it? Reflect on your answers and we will discuss them tomorrow night. I don't want you to see this trip as an event to check off. I want you to see the purpose behind it, and hold onto what you learned when we return."

John Maxwell says, "Experience isn't the best teacher. Evaluated experience is the best teacher." God uses events in our lives to teach us, bring us to maturity, and prepare us for what's next in our lives. In reflection, we wrestle with those events to wring out our purpose and calling.

So, why did God bring me here? The first answer to jump into my mind was God called me here to bring Stephanie. All her life, Stephanie wanted to come to Africa to take care of the people here. Her life's dream came true during this trip in an awesome way. I watched her interact with the children and other Ugandans and was amazed. I saw her touch her purpose in life and do what she was put on earth to do. Her gentle demeanor and caring attitude came across in a natural and confident way as she stepped into her roles. It was beautiful to watch her light up and come alive.

As I continued to ponder Bishop's question, I knew God also wanted me to step into my own strengths, gifts, and abilities. I fought against this at times, trying to act and perform in certain ways because I thought it was expected. When I let go of living up to expectations and instead followed the guidance of the Spirit, I felt fulfilled.

I came to Uganda assuming I would make a difference through providing medical care. While I know our treatment changed lives, I believe the real reason God brought me here was to change me. I didn't want to return the same person who arrived. I didn't want to waste the experience.

I learned to ask myself these questions as I walk through life. What does God want me to learn? What skill is He trying to develop? What is He preparing me to do next? God works through all situations. We just need to see it.

Everything we experience has the opportunity to shape us; the key is how we respond to various life events. A promotion at work may seem positive, but how do you respond to it? Many men use their new found authority to swagger around the office as proof of their success. Or maybe they spend their raise on a bigger house, using it as a mark of status and validation. Some of them turn the job into an escape hatch to use for areas of their life where success doesn't come easily, like helping with the kids' homework or spending time with their wives. A positive event can have a negative outcome based on the response.

And I know so many men who have suffered through trials and come out stronger and with a purpose. They never had a father growing up, so they commit to being a father figure in another child's life. Marriages suffer the damage of an affair and find forgiveness, love, and renewal the couple never thought possible. Men who experienced abuse in a variety of ways help other men find the reality and truth of the love of God.

We look at the events in our lives through God's filter. Romans 8:28 states this promise (HCSB): "We know that all things work together for the good of those who love God; those who are called according to His purpose." Our struggles have meaning. Our trials have purpose. God will work things out for good in my life, even if I don't see it. I just need to trust Him.

I struggled to find answers to these questions. I knew my life had purpose during our time in Uganda. How could I take that purpose home with me? How could I find meaning and calling in a world full of distraction? I wrestled with these questions late into the night.

The next morning started early as we gathered in the lobby, bleary-eyed and quiet, searching for the coffee like it was oxygen needed to breathe. We loaded our vehicles to go on safari in the pre-dawn darkness. We drove into the safari park and the sun rose in the sky, revealing a stunning scene overflowing with life. Herds of the deer-like animals were everywhere. A couple hyenas shambled across the road in front of us. Every time he saw a warthog, our guide would call out "Pumba!" Water buffalo gathered together in large groups as we drove past. In slow motion, giraffes strolled across distant hilltops or reached out to the top of the trees for their breakfast. Elephants, twice as big as our car and dark gray against the verdant green of the landscape, moved with casual grace and immense power through the underbrush. We made our way to the water where the hippos relaxed in their natural environment. Bouncing along the roads, we did our best to hang on and enjoy the view.

The variety of landscapes was breathtaking, and we gasped with every new vista around a turn or over a hill. We were transported from sweeping grasslands down to sandy watering holes and back to jungles thick with vegetation. I stood up in my seat to get an unobstructed view of our surroundings through the hatch in the roof. This position worked well when we stopped to look at some animals. As soon as we started driving, bouncing and swerving on the road, my ribs and back would crash into the edge of the roof. I didn't want to puncture a lung or paralyze myself, so I climbed on the roof, holding on to the rails as we bounced around.

After a couple hours of eating dust, we found the lions. Our vehicle crept through the open part of a field like a predator hunting its prey. With a shout, our guide slammed down the accelerator as two lionesses burst out of the bushes. I almost flipped over backward as we tried to keep up. These giant cats moved with effortless speed and crossed the road well ahead of our attempt to turn them back. Chests heaving with the thrill of the chase, we watched until they disappeared in the bush.

After the excitement of the safari, we had some downtime until after lunch. I couldn't wait to submerge myself in the cool water of the pool. The heat from my body dissipated as I floated on my back, looking into the azure sky. I noticed a solar halo, a rainbow ring around the sun. I had never seen one before and absorbed the beauty of God's creation as I rested.

Later in the day, we enjoyed more natural wonders when we floated up the Nile to Murchison Falls. Pods of hippos huddled in the water, trying to stay cool during the heat of the day. Crocodiles as big as kayaks lay hidden in the grass on the banks. Elephants stomped through the trees to get to the river's edge.

The birds were the most beautiful and interesting of all the animals. I loved seeing the kingfisher, who would somehow hover completely still in the air before diving toward the water in an attempt to catch a fish. The ruby-throated bee-eater is a delicate and beautiful green bird barely bigger than my thumb. While it was green on the outside, all the colors of the rainbow appeared when it opened its wings to fly. The trees were full of weaverbird nests, balls made of sticks and grass hanging in the leaves. The diversity and beauty overwhelmed the senses. My head swiveled without stopping as I tried to see everything.

We arrived at the dock and disembarked to begin our hike up to Murchison Falls. Before long, sweat was dripping from my face with the effort of the climb and the heat of the day. To distract me from the heat and strain of the walk, I sang to myself. It was a chorus I used to sing while I was growing up. "My God is so big, so strong and so mighty. There's nothing my God cannot do."

The same God created the majestic falls and the ferocious crocodile. He designed the tiny bee-eater, as well as the giant hippos and enormous elephants. The Creator of all of this sent His Son to die so that I might have a relationship with Him. Gratitude filled my heart with every beat as I absorbed the beauty of creation and felt loved by the One who created it all.

Breathless, dirty, and sweating, I arrived at the top and surveyed the scene around me. The Nile River thundered over the falls with staggering power. The mist floated from the falls and turned everything it touched a dark lush green. I was once again amazed with the power and beauty of creation.

Much too soon, it was time to load on to the bus and face our final night together. A few minutes into our journey, everyone started shouting to close the windows. We were driving through tsetse fly country. You might wonder, "What's the big deal? They're just flies." When tsetse flies smell humans, they swarm, and their bites feel like either getting punched or bitten by a horse. Either way, we did not want them to get in the bus. Even though the windows were closed, we could still see the tsetse flies trying to get in, bouncing off the windows, flying just outside. Beth told a story about the time a bus in front of them had left their windows down. It looked like a cloud enveloped the bus. They slammed on the brakes as the people poured out of the bus, arms flailing in response to the tsetse fly attack. We triple checked the windows to make sure they were closed, and we prayed the flies didn't find a way inside.

As we drove to the ferry, I stared out the window. I sensed God wasn't done with our group just yet. In spite of all the amazing scenes I had already witnessed, I prayed He would show us something awesome. I kept watch on the woods as we drove, but didn't see anything. As we pulled up to the ferry, I sighed and figured I was wrong.

We unloaded the bus to board the ferry. We milled around as the vehicles drove onto the ferry, and saw an elephant emerge from the trees on the other side of the river near the landing. A murmur went through the crowd as everyone pointed. I hoped it would wait for us to cross, but anticipated the ferry's noise would chase it off.

I was wrong. Cameras clicked as we approached the shore and the elephant stayed where it was, eating from the trees. As soon as the gate opened, we dashed off the ferry, eager to take advantage of this opportunity. In the dimming light of dusk, we took "elephant selfies," pictures of ourselves with the elephant in the background. Sam begged us to get back on the bus. "Elephants are very dangerous animals. Please come," he said. His eyes were wide with fear and he only relaxed when we were all safely on board. A huge smile crossed my face as I thanked God for this gift. My Father showed up in a remarkable way.

After dinner, we gathered in the conference room for our final debrief. Tears filled my eyes as I realized how much I did not want to leave. The remarkable experience was coming to a close and I couldn't do anything to stop it, or even to slow it down.

Around the room, the group members shared what this trip meant to them and what they wanted to take back. I struggled to find what I wanted to say. How could I put the last two weeks into a few comments? My mind whirled with the challenge.

"I have so many thoughts right now, I have no idea what is going to come out. Many of you already said some of the things bouncing around in my head." I compared the waterfall to the story of the gospel. "As we walked up to the waterfall, the land was brown and dusty. When we arrived at the falls, everywhere the water touched was green and growing. In the same way, everywhere Jesus reaches, we see growth in dry situations. I hope that everywhere we went, we left behind life."

I finally found my answer to the second question. "What will I take back? The image of my hands with nail holes as I touched people. During our clinics, I prayed to see with the eyes of Jesus and be his hands and feet to a desperate world. Well, that desperate world doesn't change when we leave Uganda. Even though we aren't in Africa, we still need to be His eyes, hands, and feet to everyone who sees us. Not just for big stuff like going to Uganda, but every day to the people in our lives."

You don't need to be in Uganda to make a difference. You can do it right now, today, in your own home. Ask God how He can use you. Look for ways for people to see Jesus in everything you do. You will be astonished at what you discover.

Stepping off the platform

Chapter 11

Follow Me

Again Jesus spoke to them, saying, "I am the light
of the world. Whoever follows me will not walk
in darkness, but will have the light of life.

- John 8:12

Have you ever ridden a zip line? It is terrifying and exhilarating all at once. Standing on a platform the size of a welcome mat. Connected to a cable no bigger than my pinky by a pair of straps cutting across a most sensitive area. Looking out over the tree tops as the breeze threatens to knock me from my perch. If I look down, the ground appears so far away my head spins. My heart pounds and my stomach jumps at the thought of stepping off the platform. My legs refuse to follow my brain's command to jump.

I gather the resilience and fortitude to make the leap. I step into the air and fall. My heart is in my throat and an uncontrolled yell escapes from my lips. White-knuckled, I grab at the harness, desperate to do anything to stop the fall. I get palpitations just thinking about it. It's a horrifying moment.

We all have platforms. Sources of stability, comfort, and security in an otherwise shaky world. Those areas where we feel strong and confident. Until the boards get pulled out from beneath us and we are flung into space, out of control and helpless.

What is your platform? Is it your job? Your family? Your brains, athletic prowess, or financial security? When everything else in your life is falling, what is the one thing you can count on?

Throughout the Bible, God asked men to step off their platforms and follow Him. Look at Abraham. In Genesis 12, God told him to leave his family, friends, and country to go to a place God would show him. Abraham obeyed and followed God, with no idea where he was going.

His great-grandson Joseph had it even worse. His brothers faked Joseph's death and sold him into slavery. He ended up in jail, but never gave up his faith. He became the second-in-command of Egypt and rescued those same brothers from dying in a famine. At the end of his life, Joseph saw God's hand in his travels. "You intended to harm me, but God intended it for good to accomplish what is now being done, the saving of many lives." (Genesis 50:20, NIV).

God called Gideon to rescue the Israelites from the oppression of the Midianites. Gideon raised an army of 32,000 men, but God told him the army was too big. How can an army be too big? God instructed him to send soldiers away until Gideon only had three hundred men. Stepping off the platform and going into battle with only three hundred soldiers was a terrifying act of faith for Gideon.

Time after time, God calls people to leave a comfortable and secure position to follow Him. Moses. David. Daniel. Jeremiah. His call continued into the New Testament.

Over and over during His ministry, Jesus gave people a simple instruction. "Follow me." They didn't know where He was going, but they dropped what they were doing to obey His call. Paul followed God to share the gospel with the Gentiles, which was unheard of in those days. If the command to follow is a consistent thread throughout the Bible, we should expect the same command to be given to us.

We are called to step out into thin air, held up as in a harness by His promises. Too often we freeze on the platform, immobilized by fear of the unknown, fear of falling and failing. During my trip to Uganda, I experienced the fear of stepping out followed by the joy of experiencing God in my calling. God is faithful to catch us and show us wonderful things when we follow Him.

Stepping off the platform and trusting the zip line is terrifying during the drop. The first step is a doozie, as they say. Until your harness catches your falling body, you are certain you will die. But once you realize you're safe in your straps, the ride becomes exhilarating. You fly through the trees like a bird, laughing and whooping. You relax because you know you're safe.

God is calling you to follow Him and jump off one of your platforms. In what area are you called to move outside your comfort zone? Step out and follow. Maybe it's trusting Him with your finances and giving the tithe. Or it could be saying no to the promotion to be more present with your family. It could even be pursuing the call to a dream that He placed in your heart.

Jumping off the platform is the first step. The Celtic Christians referenced the Holy Spirit as the "wild goose" and, many times, following God seems like a wild-goose chase. We never know what twists and turns we will endure along the way. He may even take us in circles, sometimes away from where we think we want to go. We get frustrated and disappointed because we aren't where we think we should be.

When the Israelites left Egypt, they didn't get directions. They followed God in a cloud and a pillar of fire until He delivered them to the Promised Land. The Psalms say God's word is a lamp unto our feet and a light unto our path. Jesus promised us we wouldn't walk in the dark, but in the light. Lamps don't illuminate very far. They do not highlight the entire route, just enough to see the next step or two. We must trust God and take each step as it comes.

We should not be surprised when we experience resistance to our calling. The thief comes to steal, kill, and destroy everything God wants for us. The enemy wants to steal our joy, destroy our peace, and kill our calling. When those attacks come, we remember what Joseph said: "What you meant for harm, God intended for good." And the words of Paul: "God works all things together for the good of those who love Him and are called according to His purpose."

Sometimes, the disciples fished all night and came up empty. When they listened to Jesus, they cast their nets one time and the catch was so great their nets broke. Jesus asked us to follow Him, and we went to Africa and became fishers of men. More than two thousand patients visited our clinics in Kampala and Gulu. We touched each person with the love of Jesus. We rejoiced with Heaven regarding 160 new believers – new brothers and sisters in Christ. By the end of the trip, our nets, our bodies, and our hearts were full to the point of breaking.

I returned with a more focused vision of God's purpose and call for my life. I saw idols in my life, those things I held too tightly, and was able to let them go. The seeds planted during those two weeks in Africa continue to bear fruit in my life. This book is one of them.

I stepped out of my comfort zone to follow His call, and I saw incredible things. Where faith is great, God does abundantly more than we ask or imagine. We are called to follow Him. How will you answer the call?

About the Author

Paul McDonald lives in Charlotte, NC and works as a writer, speaker, and teacher. He married Stephanie in 2010, and their blended family includes 4 children and 3 dogs. He enjoys golfing, reading, and sitting by the fire drinking a scotch while smoking a cigar. Paul shares the story of what Jesus has done in his life and wants others to experience freedom and healing through Christ.

Printed in the United States
By Bookmasters